The Art of Being

*Finding Purpose
in the Presence*

TREVOR WILLIAM HORN

The Art of Being

Finding Purpose
in the Presence

THE ART OF BEING

ISBN: 9798597991375
Independently Published

Design & author photo by Hilary Horn
Edited by Emily Croston

Printed in the United States of America 2021

To my first love.

If you like this book, tell your friends!
Tag Trevor @trevwilliamhorn
#TheArtofBeing

CONTENTS

INTRODUCTION **PANTS IN A PANDEMIC**   1

PROLOGUE **FIRST LOVE**   9

PART ONE: THE ISSUE

CHAPTER ONE **2 DEGREES**   27

CHAPTER TWO **SCROLLING**   49

PART TWO: THE INVITATION

CHAPTER THREE **FATHER**   77

CHAPTER FOUR **TELOS**   107

CHAPTER FIVE **PRESENCE**   131

EPILOGUE **HERE AND NOW**   151

CONCLUSION **2020**   161

THANKS   168

DISCUSSION   172

NOTES   181

ABOUT   203

"IF YOU WANT TO BUILD A SHIP, DON'T DRUM UP PEOPLE TO COLLECT WOOD AND DON'T ASSIGN THEM TASKS AND WORK, BUT RATHER TEACH THEM TO LONG FOR THE ENDLESS IMMENSITY OF THE SEA."

Antoine de Saint-Exupéry

Pants in a Pandemic

So I put on *pants*.

I know.
It was a BIG day.
My wife was in complete shock. I put pants on!

(* By the way, this is also what my 3 year old yells
when he dresses himself. They are almost always on
backwards but hey, he's getting after it)

Okay, some context is in order. I put on pants in the
middle of a global pandemic, which is a bit of a big
deal. Living through COVID-19, you know what
I'm talking about. If you work in the pants industry,
you especially feel these hard times. I have worked
at home for the better part of a year, meaning that
pants are not a guaranteed part of the dress code.
Who needs pants for endless Zoom calls?

I never would have guessed that putting on pants
would become such a statement, but I guess living
through a global pandemic causes one to consider
all the basic realities that we take for granted. Little

things like seeing actual living and breathing people in person or being able to breathe without some sort of face covering (and then subsequently having to inhale your own smelly breath). Ahh, good times.

But seriously - if a global pandemic causes us to rethink wearing pants, what about the deeper existential realities? The big stuff like one's purpose in the cosmos or finding the perfect picture for your online dating profile (the latter may be a step below one's core purpose on Earth, but it's a close second). The big cosmic questions that we could normally put off but have been thrust upon us in a moment of great upheaval. Questions like:

What is the good life?
What is our ultimate aim as humans?
What is the end to which we are created?

Deep questions that every human has to be able to answer to find purpose and meaning. The sort of questions that help us make sense of a merciless and chaotic world. The sort of questions that can lift our eyes and fill us with *hope*.

Hope.

A word that we all desperately need.
A word that is intricately tied into learning to *be*.

Learning to be. What a conception in the midst of COVID-19. We all have had a lot of free time these days, yet having so much time has revealed a deep issue and desperation within our own souls. We binged everything on Disney+ and dropped a ton of cash to order that Peloton® bike we always wanted. Even so, there still seems to be a deep sense of inadequacy and unfulfillment found within. If any reality has become clear in this cultural moment, it is the revealing of the deep necessity in our souls for something or someone more.

Blaise Pascal, the 17th century mathematician, physicist, and theologian, wrote an entire work on this concept of what happens when humans are forced to just be. He prophetically wrote, "Take away their diversions and you will see them bored to extinction. Then they feel their nullity without recognizing it, for nothing could be more wretched than to be intolerably depressed as soon as one is reduced to introspection with no means of diversion." [1] Tell us how you really feel, Blaise. Diversion and depression gloriously linked, walking hand-in-hand through the constant temptation to keep scrolling. To fill every waking second with Words with Friends, Snapchatstreaks and hilarious TikTok videos so that we never have to deal with the real state of our own souls. Our souls that are eroded by constant bombardment and cheap thrills, never allowing us to just be.

But what would modern people be without our constant distractions and diversions? As Pascal gracefully put it....

> ....the only thing that consoles us for our miseries is diversion. And yet it is the greatest of our miseries. For it is that above all which prevents us thinking about ourselves and leads us imperceptibly to destruction. But for that we should be bored, and boredom would drive us to seek some more solid means of escape, but diversion passes our time and brings us imperceptibly to our death.[2]

Diversion....brings us imperceptibly to our death.
What a life when diversion and distraction are the only realities that can comfort the human soul. Something we know to be true as COVID-19 has

stripped our dependence on external realities and revealed what was really happening in our inner lives.

A reality that is *the* reason that we are so unfulfilled. Pascal brings all this home with his famous line, "I have discovered that all the unhappiness of men (and women)[3] arises from one single fact, that they cannot stay quietly in their own chamber."[4] *The root of all unhappiness is that we cannot stay quietly in our own chamber.*

We could probably say it more like this: The root of all unhappiness is the inability to just *be*. Our total inability to be able to just....

Be present.
Be at peace.
Be ourselves.

Just *be*.

Forever destined to scroll. What a world. Actually, it sounds a lot like the world we currently inhabit. Where do we even begin to cross the chasm to this foreign and distant land called being? In this question lies the crux of *The Art of Being*. A work that God started in me long before COVID-19 as it has been the journey of my own soul before it was ever about any of you. A work that speaks to the deep need arising in and out of our cultural moment.

I pray that this work would in great humility and honesty unveil the deep issues within us and point each of us to the great invitation of God to learn the sacred art of being.

To reorient our lives around the presence of God.
To relearn communion with our Creator.
To learn to put on *pants* once again.

First Love

Confession time.

Time for some REAL talk. The sort of conversation that makes *The Bachelor* worth watching. Other than that guy of course. Yeah, that guy who we all know is only placed on the show for all the world to corporately hate.

(* I can't believe I am starting my first book out by talking about *The Bachelor*. Well, friends, this is going to be entertaining to say the least)

Now, onto how I messed my whole life up and lost what mattered most. *I remember when I lost my first love.* Yeah, I said it. I lost my first love (don't worry, this story is not about my wife and me. We're still happily in love).

Ah, you know first love well or you wish you knew it better (cheers, my single friends....especially my *super* single friends). No matter where you stand on your social media relationship status, I just want you to remember or imagine with me the experience of first love. Think about all the things you did when you first fell in love or just go binge watch the newest season of *The Bachelor* for a reference point. Mainly Chris Harrison always being present, tons of other contestants you're competing with, every second videotaped and every week there are cuts. Point being, just imagine that period of first love (and if necessary, do it while eating an entire pint of Ben & Jerry's. That is totally acceptable at any point in this book).

Fairly quickly into first love, it becomes readily apparent that these two star struck lovers have to be with each other every second of every day. There's not a moment that you don't want to be with that person. It's disgusting how much you want to be with that person no matter what (insert vomit emoji here). You do crazy things like....

....having to touch each other at all times (which I promise will fade by the 2nd kid. My wife and I love space nowadays and the occasional shoulder graze in bed is as risque as it gets).

....spending exorbitant amounts of time or money on that person. Attempts at making mom's famous

chicken noodle soup from scratch, hours spent
trying to find that adorable laugh out loud GIF,
organic gluten-free flowers (no idea if this is a thing,
but it sounds really expensive and very Seattle). No
cost is too high, no store is too far and nothing is
out of reach (I have yet to figure out where young
adults get all those wads of cash when they start
dating but whatevs).

….texting, snapchatting and scrolling through each
other's social media at all times of the day. Don't act
like you don't know what I'm talking about. Like,
you think you have a thing called *boundaries*. Yeah,
right….you need the dopamine hit just like I do.
Scrolling through your first love's social media is
a basic necessity of 21st century love (other than
meeting on Tinder, of course).

It is undeniable when you get in the gravitational
pull of first love. A love that is passionate, exuberant,
and what usually gets two people into a long-term
relationship in the beginning.

But over the years, something happens as these
two once star crossed lovers slowly and steadily
grow apart. A growing apart that is not usually the

result of some dramatic existential moment but a manifestation of little things over a long period of time that slowly but surely erodes the fertile soil of first love.

Little issues that grow, expand and enlarge. Distraction at the dinner table with no authentic connection. Scrolling for years at night in bed with no real conversation. Apathy that leads two former star-crossed lovers to soberly declare to the world in a Facebook post, "we *fell* out of love." Fell. Hmmm. Such strange verbiage.

I think it seems strange to me because fell sounds so accidental. Sort of like it just "happened." One day Mr and Mrs so-and-so just woke up and realized that this entire thing they were doing the last 30 years was a complete and utter sham. Too bad. No one's fault. Just fell and got stuck without a Life Alert bracelet (seriously, I may need to get one of these very soon because my late 20's are hitting me hard).

Just *fell*. Yeah, I'm not sure about this language. It just seems....

....so uncontrollable.

....so deterministic.

....so hopeless.

Maybe we need to use a different word. I think what would be more accurate is the word *lost*. At least if it's lost, then there is a chance it could be found.

Okay, take two. These two former star-crossed lovers soberly declare to the world in a Facebook post, "we lost love." That seems more appropriate. They lost the very flames that set the whole forest ablaze. Well, I guess I shouldn't say "they," like this reality is somewhere out there in the multiverse. I should bring us back to the point that started this whole conversation....*I remember when I lost my first love.*

A day that came after a long season of no boundaries and no limits. A day that came after having two kids under two (another reason why we touch less these days....and all my parents with young kids heartily declared AMEN). A day that came after birthing a third kid called a church plant who was demanding 12-14 hour work days to just sustain in a sprawling urban city. A day that came after years of late nights and early mornings trying to finish my third degree. A day that came after years of trying to burn the candle at both ends in an attempt to draw some semblance of meaning and value in my life. A day that came in Hawaii.

I remember *the* day like it was yesterday. My wife and I arrived in Hawaii for two weeks of vacation and we did what any upstanding, responsible adults do with no children....sleep. Yeah, you thought I was going to say another s-word. Nope, not on this trip, unfortunately (this is not an episode of *The Bachelor in Paradise*, my friend). We literally slept for almost two weeks straight.

We were depleted.
We were distracted.
We were depressed.

So, we slept (napping is a deeply spiritual practice, by the way). I know this sounds a bit ridiculous considering that the story so far involves:

1) Hawaii.
2) Naps.
3) No Kids.
4) Did I say Hawaii?

I know.

To get it, you really have to understand who I am
or (better yet) *who I was*. I've never been good
at this whole concept that people call being (I
know, the title of this book is quite ironic). By
nature or nurture, I am a complete doer (if you
figure out which one, let me know. I promise that
my counselor has tried). I am the hired gun you
bring in to GET STUFF DONE. I am a type
A, Enneagram 3 driver, whose favorite word is
efficiency (I am the LIFE of the party. I have five
planners with me at all times). So, it would be
safe to say that being has never been my strength
– almost as safe as the 100% chance that you're
halfway through that pint of Ben & Jerry's by now.

Hence, why two weeks in Hawaii with my own
soul was absolutely terrifying. I mean, what was
I supposed to do? I was stuck on an island with
no computer, no planner and an abundance of
pineapple (not exactly sure how pineapple relates
with the first two). After two weeks of this I realized
that after a long season of running with no limits
(actually, it was more like a lifetime), my soul was
shrinking.

I was depleted.

I was distracted.

I was depressed.

In this very place and space, I made an attempt at just being. Just for a mere moment when the heavens opened and I attempted to step off the hamster wheel I had been running on my entire life. Not days or hours but a mere moment where I stopped trying to earn something and began to learn to *be*.

What a historic moment. Insert applause here for this (recovering) performer. For 30 minutes I just sat in one place with no attempt at outward achievement. It was probably more like 10 minutes since the first 20 minutes were me plotting strategies in my planners for being….and my future presidential campaign, of course. What a novel concept, to just be.

Would you believe that God actually met me in that moment? I can't say it was dramatic or that the heavens opened and an angel came down. Surprisingly, God's voice in this moment sounded more like a cool, quiet whisper that could only be heard if one decided to just be. In this quiet whisper He spoke words that cut me deeper than any words I had heard before or will ever hear.

Words that cut soul and spirit.
Words that caused me to mourn.
Words that brought me to my knees.

In the quiet of the cool, afternoon, Edenic-like breeze; God whispered so gracefully to me,

"Trevor, you have lost your *first love*."

I had lost the only love that mattered. But how could this have happened? How did I go from purely a lover to a worker?

I….me….yeah, that guy who gave his entire life to the ministry of his Lord had lost his first love. I got in this whole ministry thing to tell people about the radical, reckless, pursuing love of God, yet I had lost my love for Him in the process? How did I come to sit in this privileged place of the saints throughout church history who flamed out and lost their love for the very presence of God (there's got to be a Hall of Fame for this)?

It felt like yesterday, when I was awoken by first love. When at summer camp, in the last evening chapel of the week, a little 7th grade punk (totally me) heard the gracious invitation of our Lord through a message of God's sacrificial love on the cross. When at that very summer camp I staggered out into the night awoken and enamored by the beauty of the Gospel. When all I could muster was to lay for hours gazing at the night's sky, desiring nothing in all of the world but to just be with my newfound Savior.

It felt like yesterday, when every word I read in scripture seemed to be written directly to me. Daily I would approach my Bible reading with faith-filled expectation and a deep, desperate hunger (even through the wild stuff like Leviticus. Don't worry, we're going there later in the book. Yes, this is the first book in human history that mentions both *The Bachelor* and Leviticus). Through thick and thin, nothing could keep me from spending my mornings reading scripture as a profound opportunity to be with God.

It felt like yesterday when all I yearned for was to spend hours talking with God. I remember waking up at 4 am in college just so I could find more time in the day to commune with my Creator (again, as you can tell, I was the life of the party in my frat with my extensive prayer times + many planners). I remember hearing the sweetness of God's voice for the first time and desiring nothing but His voice to lead the way in every aspect of my life.

It felt like yesterday that nothing in the whole world could keep me from just being with God. Yet now I struggled to spend 30 minutes just being with Him (again, it was more like 10 minutes of actual being and 20 minutes in a business meeting format around #Horn2024). Maybe this is why people say they fell out of love. They can't seem to find one moment or turning point where they could remember when it all just unraveled. It just happened.

Day by day.
Month by month.
Year by year.
Decade by decade.

They just *fell*. But again, if it isn't necessarily that they fell but that it's just lost then maybe there is a chance to find this first love once again.

To rekindle a holy desire.

To rediscover a passion for the divine.

To reorient back to the very presence of God.

To retrace one's steps back to the very place where first love began.

Actually, I remember our premarital counselors talking to Hilary and me about something like this. They had told us that if we ever found ourselves in this place to retrace our steps and merely do what we did in the beginning (all the gushy and gross stuff I mentioned earlier).

More hilarious GIFs.

More *Bachelor* episodes.

More social media scrolling.

More of what led to first love.

But the Jesus-sy version of this. So all I had to do to rekindle first love was….

….more early morning prayer sessions.

….more late night star-gazing with God.

….more Leviticus (sort of like more cowbell).

….more presidential campaign planning (oh wait, maybe that doesn't fit with this list. Remember, I'm a recovering performer).

....more time just being with my *first love*.

§

It has been years now since that fateful day in
Hawaii, but it hasn't lost its power or potency in my
life. It serves for me as a mile marker on my journey
with God where I had to reorient and relearn
communion with our Creator.

Yet here I stand. I'm not perfect. Some days I spend
my mornings trying to think through #Horn2024
(especially in our current cultural climate). It's less
often these days, though. More often than not I
grab my morning coffee in my mug, sit in my chair
and take time to just be with God. It's not complex,
it's not mystical and it's actually quite simple (sorry,
I'm not cool enough to be your guru or get a new
agey Netflix documentary). Just me and God (as
well as my two little crazies who really like waking
up at 3:59 AM....more to come on this). Nothing
more, nothing less.

It was not even that I had to necessarily do more
to rediscover my first love as it was more so that
I lost the very connection of the various spiritual

practices I was doing in relation to the presence of God. Dallas Willard, a legend on the topic of spiritual formation, writes in his classic work, *The Spirit of the Disciplines*: "Yet when we look closely and continually at Jesus, we do not lose sight of this one fundamental, crucial point—the activities constituting the disciplines *have no value in themselves.* The aim and substance of spiritual life is not fasting, prayer, hymn singing, frugal living, and so forth. Rather, it is the effective and full enjoyment of active love of God and humankind in all the daily rounds of normal existence where we are placed." [1]

The activities constituting the disciplines have no value in themselves. All of the spiritual disciplines and practices are central, but they only help when they are put in their proper place, which is the Presence. This is vital because even doing tons of good and godly things can burn us out when they're not placed in alignment with being with God. An all to common lifestyle that is built on becoming like God and doing things for Him while forgetting the radical invitation of being with Him as our primary aim.

So with this in mind, I invite you. Yes, I invite *you*.[2] Not who you think you should be or who you were told to be. Just you who is imperfect, super single, prone to incessant distraction and loves to binge watch *The Bachelor* (with pints of ice cream on hand). Just you who feels completely inadequate to broach the subject of being yet at the same time is one who is infinitely loved and accepted by a God who just wants to be with you.

An invitation….
….to be able to rediscover *first love.*
….to be able to recalibrate *2 degrees* at a time.
….to be able to stop *scrolling* and focus on our true *Father.*
….to be able to know the very *telos* we were created for in the *Presence*.
….to be able to learn the art of being in the *here and now.*

Learning to discover that **the fundamental goal of our lives is to "be" with God**. The central truth that helped me rediscover and rekindle my own first love. With these truths in mind, let's journey together, with clear eyes and full hearts, to learn the art of being and the deep *issue* at work.

Part One:

The Issue

2 Degrees

In 1914, not long after the sinking of the *Titanic*, Congress convened a hearing to discuss what happened in another nautical tragedy. In January of that year, in the thick fog off the Virginia coast, the steamship *Monroe* was rammed by the merchant vessel *Nantucket* and eventually sank. Forty-one sailors tragically lost their lives in the frigid winter waters of the Atlantic that day.

While it was Captain Osmyn Berry of the *Nantucket* who was brought in on charges, in the course of the trial Captain Edward Johnson of the *Monroe* was grilled on the stand for over five hours. *The New York Times* would report from the hours of cross examination:

> Captain Johnson navigated the Monroe with a steering compass that deviated as much as two degrees from the standard magnetic compass. He said the instrument was sufficiently true to run the ship, and that it was custom of masters in the coastwise trade to use such compasses. His steering compass had never been adjusted

in the one year he was the master of the Monroe.[1]

What happened to Captain Johnson was not uncommon for seamen of his day. Slowly but surely, his navigational compass lost its ability to track the earth's magnetic north. The faulty compass that seemed adequate for navigation eventually proved to be off by 2 degrees, leading to disaster.

This story is not just about a tragic loss of life, but the tragic consequences of being a little off over a long period of time. Simply 2 degrees here or there. Little decisions, day-in and day-out, that dramatically affect the outcome of one's life over the years.

We see the tragic results of being 2 degrees off all the time. Think of the latest pastor you've heard of, or maybe even personally know, who had some sort of moral failure (using pastors since I am a pastor. You could easily insert your celeb of choice in here as well). If I were to guess, I would say it was probably one of big three that got him or her: power, sex or money. He went on a power trip and bulldozed over his staff. She went on a spending spree with last weekend's offering and made it on Preachers n' Sneakers (if you don't know what this is, well, just look it up on Instagram). He shacked up with his assistant and is currently living in an adulterous relationship, breaking up his "perfect" family of four.

Now, think about the very moment you heard the news. The first thing I hear people say all the time is, *how could he do that?* Sheer disbelief and shock settles into our souls, yet we miss the tragic cautionary tale for our own spiritual lives. We think this blatant sin just "happened."

So-and-so was just walking by and the idea popped into his head to ruin his career, marriage and family all in one fatal swoop. Might as well go big or go home. If you're going to sin, you may as well *really* sin. Go to Vegas and get it all out of the way, Prodigal Son style.

Maybe that last part went a little far (just maybe), yet this flawed thought process of sin just "happening" drastically misses the root of the disaster itself. If we are off in our discipleship, it often does not begin with some grievous sin but with a few degrees off here or there over a long period of time.

Years of unforgiveness and bitterness building up. Years of consistently pushing beyond one's capacity. Years of scrolling through social media with unbridled lust. Years of moving from job to job refusing to submit to authority.

Do I need to keep going? *The seeds of our own destruction are ever present in the habits of our daily lives.*

Building.
Growing.
Multiplying.

Russian novelist and Nobel prize winner, Aleksandr Solzhenitsyn, while living through the days of the Soviet Union and communist regime had this realization of where this ever-present danger really lies. He understood that:

> Gradually it was disclosed to me that the line separating good and evil passes not through states, nor between classes, nor between

political parties either -- but right through
every human heart -- and through all human
hearts. This line shifts. Inside us, it oscillates
with the years. And even within hearts
overwhelmed by evil, one small bridgehead of
good is retained. And even in the best of all
hearts, there remains....an unuprooted small
corner of evil.[2]

*Right through every human heart....an unuprooted
small corner of evil.* The great issues plaguing our age
are not "out there" but dwelling in you and me right
now. The chief issue facing our age is not global
warming, tensions in the middle east or who our
current president is.[3] *The chief issue in our day is that
our hearts are broken compasses that long for their true
north in God.*

Our hearts crave direction.
Our hearts desire the divine.
Our hearts desperately need God.

Leading to the necessity of regular recalibration
through being with God. A type of recalibration
that is deeply correlated to our daily habits and
spiritual practices. The sort of stuff my Seattleite

friends and I do in our local coffee shop every morning while sipping on our guji in beanies and Birkenstocks, reading Leviticus (Yes, this is a type of coffee....not the other type of "guji" popular in Seattle).[4]

Day-by-day.
Week-by-week.
Year-by-year.

Or, as Eugene Peterson aptly called it, "a long obedience in the same direction."[5] Daily habits and disciplines that help form us to our true north as well as fight the deformative power of our cultural moment 2 degrees at a time. Displaying the intimately connected and correlated process of the presence of God and our daily practices.

A process that is the key component of our spiritual growth as we continually immerse ourselves in stories. Stories that are key for understanding what we were created for and what we are to do. Alasdair MacIntyre famously wrote to this end, "I can only answer the question 'What am I to do?' if I can answer the prior question 'Of what story or stories do I find myself a part?'"[6] What we are to do is deeply embedded in the story or stories that we believe about humanity and the world. Therefore leading to the importance of not just understanding stories but *the story* which explains our true origin as humans.

The story to which all other stories are merely a shadow. *The story* that brings us to the root of our shared humanity. *The story* that has been told and retold for a millennia across cultures and continents. *The story* that takes us back to a garden called Eden.

§

Genesis 3:1-5 // Now the serpent was more crafty than any other beast of the field that the Lord God had made. He said to the woman, "Did God actually say, 'You shall not eat of any tree in the garden'?" And the woman said to the serpent, "We may eat of the fruit of the trees in the garden, but God said, 'You shall not eat of the fruit of the tree that is in the midst of the garden, neither shall you touch it, lest you die.'" But the serpent said to the woman, "You will not surely die. For God knows that when you eat of it your eyes will be opened, and you will be like God, knowing good and evil."

"In the beginning...."[7]

The place where all good stories begin. On the scene in this story is not a prince or princess but "God." A God who is an artist painting "the heavens and the earth."[8] A God who is forming and filling the land, culminating in the creation of humans as His divine image bearers. The immensity and complexity of what we could cover on page one of the Bible is overwhelming, to say the least, but let's begin with one key observation.

Genesis 1 and Genesis 2-3 are strange because they seem to be telling the same story. I don't know about you, but when I first started reading the Bible, I read Genesis 1 and was like, "Oh I get it, God creates everything." But then I got to Genesis 2 and it felt sort of like a rerun. Didn't God already create humans and plants in Genesis 1? Maybe the author used all of his best stuff in Chapter 1 so he had to tell the same stories again (what a bummer. Who was this person's publisher?).[9]

Yet what if the repetition was actually key? A mark of sheer brilliance with an artist at work as Genesis opens with two complementary accounts about God's creative work. Genesis 1 is the zoom out lens of the creation narrative. It gives us the picture of this transcendent, sovereign deity who creates all. Then, Genesis 2-3 zooms in on the intimate details of God's creative work with His image bearers (humans) through their calling to work and the covenant of marriage. Point being, God is both CEO and sculptor.

A picture that becomes readily clear when we pay attention to the intricate details of how the narrative describes God. All throughout Genesis 1, we see God described as, well, "God" or in Hebrew, *Elohim*. We see:

God saw.
God said.
God made.
God called.
God created.
God blessed.[10]

He is giving Ted Talks, snapchatting, bird watching, papier-mâchéing and making it rain dollar bills all at the same time. He's multifaceted and boundless in chapter 1, or as theologians refer to Him, *transcendent*.

But something changes in chapters 2-3 as God has a different name. Now He is not referred to as only "God" but as "the Lord God" or in Hebrew; *Yahweh Elohim*. We see:

The Lord God formed the man.
The Lord God caused a deep sleep to fall upon the man.
The Lord God planted a garden….and there he put the man.
The Lord God took the man and put him in the garden of Eden to work and keep it.[11]

God is playing with playdough, planting pineapple trees, assigning labor and giving the man a tempurpedic mattress to name a few things. We see God intimately working with our ancestors throughout Genesis 2-3, or put another way, we see His *immanence*. And in this contrast is the point of the complementary pictures of God in Genesis 1-3.

God is both *transcendent* and *immanent*. [12] We
know this to be true. In one sense, we know God
is busy running the world as the sovereign ruler of
all. If you don't know what I'm talking about, just
watch *Bruce Almighty* and you'll get the picture (you
should definitely imagine the rest of this chapter
being read by Morgan Freeman). This narrative
makes it evident that God is wholly sovereign but
at the same time deeply personal. God desires a
relationship with all 7 billion humans on Earth,
including you and I.

He seeks us.
He desires us.
He is absolutely crazy about us.
He wants to start a conversation with each of
us today. Yet He is not the only one who desires
to reveal Himself in this opening story of the
scriptures.

We also are told of a serpent who was "more crafty
than any other beast of the field." *Crafty* is quite
an interesting word to add because most stories in
the Hebrew Bible do not insert words to describe
characters in the middle of the narrative. Usually,
they let the story play out and let us as the reader

make a judgment on the characters themselves. When the narrator inserts a key character trait like crafty, we are to pay close attention to the subtleness of what the serpent will say as it serves as a narrative key for the reader. To be clear, the word crafty (*arum*) doesn't inherently imply the serpent is a good or bad figure but again that we need to pay close attention to the subtleness of the serpent's words in the narrative to determine the character and nature of the serpent.[13]

(* Speaking of subtleness - yes, this is a snake speaking. My running theory is that Adam and Eve could speak Parseltongue and were actually Slytherins. A key theological lesson for us and the reason why homeschool parents don't let their kids read *Harry Potter* + drink the guji)

As the serpent reveals himself, notice not just what he says but whom he speaks to. We are told, "He said to the woman…." The serpent is speaking to one of God's original creations: the woman, aka Eve. But it's *just* Eve. No Adam. Think about that. What was Adam doing? Drinkin' the guji with his friends? Watchin' the big game? The woman had just been created. This relationship is fresh and we all know how gross people in new relationships are. We were just told that they are to "hold fast" to one another and become "one flesh."[14] Yet the serpent only speaks to one of the covenant partners, isolating Eve from her most vital relational connections. I am not saying that Eve needed a big strong man around because we all know Adam would have been way too easy of a target. The serpent needed a real challenge as his schemes are always born *in the fertile soil of isolation.*

Isolation from friends.
Isolation from wise counsel.
Isolation at the hands of one's iPhone.

Overconnected digitally but under connected with real, flesh and blood relationships. Living in an echo chamber of our own thoughts, ideas and YouTube browser. The place where we always make our best choices (yeah, not really).

After isolating one of God's creations, the serpent speaks one of the most profound questions in human history: *Did God actually say?* He opens not with an overtly blatant falsehood or degrading remark about God but a question. A question that makes a profound theological statement. As the serpent refers to God, notice the name he uses for God. Throughout this whole of Genesis 2-3, we see the personal name of God being used, *Yahweh Elohim.*

God is present.
God is involved.
God is attentive.

Yet the serpent is the first character in these chapters to merely refer to God as God, or *Elohim.* The serpent refuses to use Yahweh, the personal name of God. He wants Eve to think, "Hmm where did God go? I know He's busy creating the world but maybe He's taken His hands off the wheel (the opposite of Jesus take the wheel….thank you, Carrie Underwood)." The serpent is attempting to unhinge the creation from their Creator. Isn't this what he does? Sometimes he tells blatant falsehoods about God, but most of the time it comes in the form of an all too subtle whisper. "What's the big deal? No one will ever know. It's just a small decision; 2 degrees at best. So, go and do you."

The serpent, the king of creating distance and

deception. A deception embedded in the second part of his question, "Did God actually say, 'You shall not eat of *any* tree in the garden?'" Is this what God actually said to humans? God had clearly articulated before this, "And out of the ground the Lord God made to spring up every tree that is pleasant to the sight and good for food....You may surely eat of *every* tree in the garden, but of the tree of knowledge of good and evil you shall not eat."[15] God graciously lavished His goodness on His creation. God gave a bazillion trees to His people to eat from and it was so "good."

Yet there was only one tree in the entire lush forest of creation that was off limits. So, the serpent focused Eve's attention not on what she had but what she didn't have - *underplaying God's blessing and overplaying God's boundaries.* Therefore shifting humans from a perspective of *sufficiency to scarcity.* The serpent knows that humans when in a scarcity mindset aren't themselves (sort of like all those Snickers commercials and how "you're not you when you're hungry"). We do crazy things when we make decisions that aren't aligned with who we are or who we were created to be. We go for the "guji" of all things (bad guji this time).

This leads humans to begin to ask questions. Eve responds to the Serpent, commenting, "We may eat of the fruit of the trees in the garden." Again, is this what God said? If you're going to quote God, you should at least make sure it's right. Notice the key word she leaves out from God's words. God had said, "You may surely eat of *every* tree of the garden."[16]

Every.

She forgets God's promise that they could eat of every tree, not merely some of the fruit. She is essentially saying, "Well, we can eat of some of the fruit. It may not be all of it but God left us something, I guess. Got to love divine leftovers. Who's doing the cooking around here?" You can see the wheels turning in her head. She is slowly beginning to minimize the gracious provision of God and all of the blessings He had laid before her and Adam.

If only it stopped there, but it doesn't. Notice how Eve refers to "God." When quoting God, she tells the Serpent, "but God said." She immediately uses the transcendent name for God instead of

His personal name that is almost exclusively used throughout chapters 2-3. *She takes the serpent's definition of God, not God's definition of Himself.* Settling for secondary sources versus going straight to the primary source of all life and love. She still believes in God but God's not as present anymore.

Uninvolved.
Uninterested.
Unconcerned.

She sees the texting bubbles pop up but no response (the worst feeling *ever*). She's losing her true north at the hands of the serpent. Slowly but surely and oh so subtly. She has become spiritual but not religious. She still has faith but doesn't really believe in the whole "institutional" thing.

This all comes to a head in Eve's final comment to the serpent. She finishes quoting God, saying, "but God said, 'You shall not eat of the fruit of the tree that is in the midst of the garden, *neither shall you touch it*, lest you die.'" Notice what she adds to God's statement. God never said she couldn't touch it. Sure, He said not to eat from it but He never said anything about touching it. Eve is beginning to add rules and laws onto what God said. Shifting her focus from the organic-ness of a real and raw relationship with God to living under mere rules from a divine buzzkill. From a loving Father to the guy who tells you not to step on wet cement (what a drag, right? We both know you want to put your hand print on that sidewalk). What a tragedy, or better said….how crafty.

At this point, the serpent boldly strikes. He swings for the fences, proclaiming to Eve, "You will not surely die. For God knows that when you eat of it your eyes will be opened." Finally, a clear and blatant lie from the serpent as God had said earlier, "you shall surely die."[17] But notice how subtle this process was. The serpent slowly but surely shifted Eve's perspective. Isn't this what he does? He slowly erodes the soil of our souls. He may not be able to get you to cast God out of the picture with blatant lies or falsehoods but he can work slowly and surely. He gets us caught up in the busyness and the noise of the world, slowly eroding our souls from the inside out.

The sort of stuff that only happens in increments of *2 degrees*. Over years and under the surface of our lives at the hands of the serpent who is *crafty*.

§

By now you're getting the *process* of how I flamed
out and how most people end up losing their
passion for (the Lord) God (in my humble opinion).
A process that happens 2 degrees at a time at the
hands of the crafty serpent. More so the opposite
of how Eugene Peterson phrased it, "A long
*dis*obedience in the same direction (that would be a
heck of a book title....it just screams "best seller")."
A long process of being a little off over a long
period of time that leads to sheer destruction.

Now I don't mean to be a complete buzzkill; 2
degrees also has a great hope embedded in it.
Recovering one's first love isn't some Herculean
effort reserved for some Avengers, save the world
moment, but a matter of recalibrating our daily
habits and practices. Little things over a long period
of time that make a world of difference. Daily time
being with God over one's morning guji that can
redirect and reset the trajectory of our entire life if
we are willing to accept the process.

(* For some reason I keep hearing Allen Iverson saying "practice" when I am writing *process*. I don't know what to do with that, but for added effect, imagine that press conference and it will help you get the importance of what I'm talking about. Or, totally just go back to reading in Morgan Freeman's voice)

So now that you know how the process of losing one's first love happens, it's time to go and practice. Go be with God. Make it happen. Just do it. Yet I think we all know that it's not that simple as we have yet to get to the core of the real *problem*. If we stripped away all the layers and got to the heart of the matter, what would be the deepest reason for our inability to just be? With this question in mind, let's take a darker turn in chapter 2.

Scrolling

3:59 AM.

That moment of absolute glory, said no one ever except me. I am fairly certain that my wife just vomited in her mouth. She takes my breath away but mornings aren't her thing. What can I say? I'm sort of a big deal. I'm not trying to play the comparison game (I totally am) but I seriously did wake up at 3:59 AM recently. This is a completely true story (well, maybe "based on a true story" is more accurate).

I guess it was under different circumstances then you may imagine. My moment of morning glory was due to a deranged and maniacal "thing" living in my home called a three year old. "It" loves to wake up his parents at ungodly hours to beat us into total and utter submission to his will. In this moment of sheer glory, you can imagine between my wife and I who got out of bed to deal with "it." You know…. daddy.

My wife and I don't even have to communicate

anymore about who gets out of bed. We hear the rustling of our baby terrorists (forgot to say, I have a two year old as well who quickly shifts from victim to accomplice). In the moment, we usually try to move as little as possible in hopes that they may think we died in our sleep (wouldn't that be easier than waking up at 3:59 AM?). Yet somehow they are never convinced by our acting (which, I do have to say, is pretty darn good). As we look at each other, all I see is the bloodshot look in my wife's eyes that clearly communicates, "If you don't get out of bed right now, I will go on a rampage and kill everyone in this house with a butter knife." So I got out of bed at 3:59 AM. Point for Trevor.

As I got out of bed, I did what any normal 21st century human does when they first wake up: I checked my iPhone (duh).[1] Now, let's imagine this morning that we're in this together because we all know that you're not better than me with this whole boundaries thing. Actually, for your sanity (and so my wife doesn't kill us all), we can make it 7:05 AM (you're welcome….and somewhat conscious now).

Take two - 7:05 AM. You're awoken from your slumber and the first thing you do is grab your iPhone from your night stand (or if you're a minimalist, the floor. Sorry, you chose the lifestyle). And what is the first thing you check on your iPhone? Social media. Duh. Next question please.

Let's say you decide to go through Instagram first this morning. You prop yourself up a bit on your pillow, taking time to check *all* your notifications. I know you're a big deal who has at least 150 followers who demand your constant attention. I get it. You're all the rage since you boldly declared your minimalist lifestyle 2 days ago. What will the world do if they don't get constant updates about your new lifestyle (#boutthatminmalistlyfe)? World War 3 may break out, so you check Insta but you have *zero* notifications.

Nada.
The worst.
Total gut check.

I had that happen to me a few weeks ago and decided to like my own photos to give myself the dopamine hit. I'm not an addict. Remember, this is about *you*. So you have no notifications, which means it's time to start *scrolling*.

The first picture you see is:

jockowillink ···

13,131 likes
jockowillink GO TIME.

Your morning motivation from ex-Navy Seal
Jocko Willink, who woke up at 3:59 AM of his
own volition (maybe he has a 3-year old too?).[2]
Seriously, that reads 3:59 AM. Pre-sun coming up.
T-minus 3 hours and 6 minutes ago. That godless
hour where nothing holy can happen. The time that
was invented by the crafty Serpent himself when
you're *finally* hitting REM sleep is when Jocko got
up and boldly declared, "GO TIME." All caps.
That's motivation. You know what, we need to keep
scrolling.

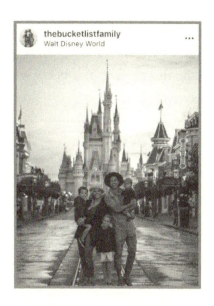

Oh, look at this! A new post from the Bucket List
Family. Oh my gosh, they are at Disneyland![3] So
much fun. Wait, what time is it? 7:23 AM. Well,
that's a little more reasonable then Jocko.

But they got their three kids under four up at 5 AM
and they took this picture by 7 AM? WITH ALL
KIDS PRESENT....SMILING....LOOKING
AT THE CAMERA. *God's Not Dead* (that movie
didn't sell me but this picture does). It's not like
my family's Christmas card last year took us about
6 hours to get one picture where both kids were
staring in the same general direction (meaning our
2 year old was looking up at the sky with his finger

straight up his right nostril....but hey, you gotta start somewhere with baby terrorists). If only our family could be this perfect. You know what, we need to keep scrolling.

OH MY GOSH! Look at this picture![4] Cassie posted on Colton's Instagram; they are the *perfect* couple. I know this was from a few seasons ago on *The Bachelor*, but I LOVE them together. I watched the whole season on TV.

(* Yes....TV. What's that, you ask? Well, sit around the campfire my Gen Z friends as I spin you a tale of old. It's sort of like Netflix or Hulu but happening live at a scheduled time every week apart from your choosing or binging delight. One episode

a week. No control. No automatic next show button.
I know. So archaic. How did people live?)

I was watching *The Bachelor* on TV and that season
was wild. Cassie turned down Colton, which led
Colton to jump over a fence and pursue her like a
stalker, but look at them now.

So perfect. Shalom.
Genesis 1-2 type stuff.
The world is the way it's supposed to be.

But I just feel so lonely. If only I had a relationship
like them (unfortunately, at the publishing of
this book, Cassie and Colton are no longer
together. Now we *really* have no hope of making
a relationship work. We're going to need a bigger
container of Ben & Jerry's, fam).

Okay, end scene. No more scrolling. Let's ask an
honest question at this point in the morning: how
are you feeling about the coming day? Like, really
feeling. Maybe you get a slight bump of morning
motivation because you're deranged like me, but
more than likely you feel behind. You woke up
excited for another day on this planet but now

you're playing the catch up game by 7:05 AM and you can't figure out why. You feel like you need to try harder.

To do more.
To become someone else.
To make something happen.

You're stuck on the proverbial social media hamster wheel with no way to get off. Is it even possible? How, in our image-obsessed, filter-based culture, do we learn to just be human? Or better yet, how do we learn to just *be*?

Be. What a novel concept. Is that something the Amish do? Maybe the minimalists? Was that something around with the whole "TV" thing? Be. Hmmm.

Actually, let's go scrolling one more time. Back into the hamster wheel because every once in a while there is a glimmer of shared hope in Hell. Yes, *hope* in the form of a Facebook post. Author Shauna Niequist posted this that so aptly described our morning together:

Shauna Niequist
3 hrs · 🌐

Some days I feel like the internet is 100 versions of "strive for greatness!" & "crush everything!" & "be all the things!" & "how she's killing the game & you can, too!" & "these are the 64863 things successful people do before dawn."

But how about this: you don't have to crush or kill or slay anything today. You don't have to strive or wrangle or hustle or do anything violent today. You can just be a human, in a quiet & honest way, & that's good too.

👍 Like   💬 Comment   ↪ Share

You can just be a human.[5] What an idea. You can just be. Today, you don't have to post the "perfect" family picture. Today, you don't have to wake up at 3:59 AM to prove to the world how great you are. Today, you don't have to find your soul mate or prove to the world how you and your spouse have it all together. You can just....*be.*

Be present.
Be at peace.
Be who you were destined to be.

What an idea. Minimalist-esque *and* an absolutely terrifying concept to the modern soul. A deep plight that philosophers and theologians have been pointing towards for hundreds of years. A point that the great encourager, Frederick Nietzsche, ever so softly tried to make (yeah, not really). The 19th century philosopher, who lamented the death of God, saw this cultural moment of incessant scrolling coming. He proclaimed,

> God is dead. God remains dead. And we have killed him. How shall we, murderers of all murderers, console ourselves? That which was the holiest and mightiest of all that the world has yet possessed has bled to death under our knives. Who will wipe this blood off us?[6]

Who will wipe this blood off us? Really dark yet profoundly tied to why we are consistently stuck scrolling *as the moment you kill the Creator, you instantly kill something deep within the creation.* Or, you kill the only One that humans can look to to truly find consolation for our souls, leading to the death of the ability to just be.

This idea of the death of God has birthed the cultural moment in which we now reside that many refer to as a secular age. Philosopher Charles Taylor in his magnum opus on how we got where we are today writes, "For the first time in history a purely self-sufficient humanism came to be a widely available option. I mean by this a humanism accepting no final goals beyond human flourishing, nor any allegiance to anything else beyond this flourishing. *Of no previous society was this true.*[7] For the first time in world history, a culture has been able to define itself on its own terms apart from the divine (cheers, we did it. Participation trophies for everyone).

We now have the ability to live our entire lives without a thought of the transcendent, living solely focused on the immanent. It really is quite remarkable in light of the rest of human history that we can live our entire lives in the natural world with no concern for something more (and can officially sleep in on Sundays guilt free).[8] No longer bound by the divine, we can now express how profoundly hopeful we are in the human project.

You think we now have a shot against global warming or nuclear holocaust with North Korea. You tweet your hopefulness to the world. You recycle your used kombucha containers to save the sea turtles. You road tripped to Standing Rock to stop the Dakota pipeline from going in (I know....

Europe was a bit too expensive so you settled for the Dakotas). You are changing the world one tweet, one kombucha, one protest at a time (let's not forget the bamboo straws as well).[9] Every moment of every day has the song "Everything is Awesome" playing in the background (thank you to *The Lego Movie* for giving us a tune to remind us of the sheer depravity of catchy children's songs).

You have declared your hopefulness for humanity to the world in 140 characters, but is this how you really feel? Deep down in your soul, do you *actually* feel hopeful or are you just tweeting your hopefulness? Resorting to incessant scrolling to dull that background song that continually plays on repeat: "Everything is (*not*) awesome."

(* To be clear, I know that Twitter now allows 280 characters, but what can I say - I am a traditionalist)

Let's just get *real* at this point. We've been walking together for a few chapters now (and neither of us have put pants on yet). I know that you do these good things, but somewhere deep within you are just like everyone else.

You feel overwhelmed by watching school shooting after school shooting and wondering when something will be done. You feel tired after hearing the doom-and-gloom predictions about how the world will end at the hands of global warming by 2049. You feel weary over the great injustices in our country as we see another headline of police brutality and are constantly reminded of the 400 years of systemic racism. You feel out of control at the hands of the bombardment of the 24/7 news cycle and constant connection at the hands of your iPhone. You are haunted by the sense that there is "something more" that you were created for.

You turned your iPhone off, moved to a tiny home and joined the minimalists for this very reason. To help settle that deep despair in your soul. But, you still feel defeated (and *still* have "Everything is Awesome" stuck in your head). Producing the regular rhythm of incessant scrolling.

Despair.
Disinterest.
Distraction.

Candy Crush and Angry Birds, born to relieve the

modern consciousness of its feeling of being utterly out of control at the hands of a merciless world. Maybe we should start scrolling again, because that was much more palatable than this.

Could there be a way out of this constant cycle of diversion and despair? Remember, Nietzsche's point was not just about our inability to console ourselves but that this lack of consolation was born from the death of God. If we brought Him back, then maybe He could bring us the counsel we so desperately need? I heard Him referred to as Mighty Counselor, and He's much cheaper to meet with than my actual counselor (love you, Marcus).[10]

What if the solution to the deep problem and plight of our secular age was not merely something unique to our modern world but in uniformity with generations of the past? Maybe we actually need solutions that are pre-Candy Crush, our iPhones and that thing called a "TV." Meaning that this whole scrolling thing is so much deeper.

Deeper than social media.
Deeper than endless scrolling.
Deeper than Cassie and Colton.

The total inability to just be is not a technology problem but a profoundly human one that unites us with our ancestors.[11] We don't just need modern approaches to hack our lives like minimalism or Marie Kondo; we need an ancient approach that addresses the deep problem of the human condition.

The problem that cuts deeper than mere flesh and blood to our hearts and souls. *The problem* that has been identified as the deep issue in our hearts for over a millennia by our ancestors. *The problem* that leads us home to the root of our shared humanity. *The problem* that brings us back to a garden called Eden.

§

Genesis 3:4-7 // But the serpent said to the woman, "You will not surely die. For God knows that when you eat of it your eyes will be opened, and you will be like God, knowing good and evil." So when the woman saw that the tree was good for food, and that it was a delight to the eyes, and that the tree was to be desired to make one wise, she took of its fruit

and ate, and she also gave some to her husband who was with her, and he ate. Then the eyes of both were opened, and they knew that they were naked. And they sewed fig leaves together and made themselves loincloths.

"Then the eyes of both were opened."

Adam and Eve could see for the first time, like a newborn opening her eyes after 9 months in the womb. What a moment. The very *first* result of our ancestors eating the fruit of the tree of the knowledge of good and evil was the ability to see? Strange. Adam's given bifocals. Doesn't seem all that profound until you realize the central place of one's "eyes" in the story of the scriptures.

There is a dark book a little later in the biblical story called Judges. It's six books to the right in our Bibles (after Genesis) and is the story of total and absolute failure in the Promised Land. This book is full of blood, murder, moral corruption, child sacrifices, the pillaging of innocent villages, rape and sexual abuse *by God's people.*[12] The people who were supposed to be completely set apart and holy are acting like the rest of the nations around them. The story of Judges culminates with a complete civil war among God's people, almost wiping out one of the twelve tribes of Israel.[13] This book is R-rated. *Captain America: Civil War*-esque, almost tearing apart the dream team. This stuff makes good television, but it's really dark (see the explanation earlier in this chapter for what a "television" is). So dark we should be wondering, how in the world did Judges make the cut?

There is one profound line in the darkness of Judges that can help us comprehend the point of it all and bring consolation to our distracted souls if we heed its fateful warning. It is repeated throughout the book of Judges and is actually the very last line of the entire book. Judges makes the profound observation, "In those days there was no king in Israel. Everyone did what was right in their own eyes."[14] Notice the connection here between two key main ideas, that there was:

1) no *king*....

....and....

2) ....people did what was right in their own *eyes*.

Two interrelated ideas, screaming to us to learn from our ancestors' mistakes and paving the way for a better future. Now, let's begin with the king part first and then come back to the idea of our eyes later.

Judges tells us that Israel had no king. Think about it, though: did Israel have a king in the time of the judges? Well, yes and no (I hate when teachers ask questions they have the answers to already. Stick with me). God's people were governed by local tribal chieftains during this time that were called judges. They were primarily regional, but in times of crisis God would raise up one of them to deliver the entire nation. But, none of them were a king.

We are told about one person, however, who was *the* central leader of the nation during those desperate days. God speaks to the prophet Samuel when the people finally beg for an earthly king and monarchy after years of disaster in the time of the judges: "Obey the voice of the people in all that they say to you, for they have not rejected you, but they have rejected me from being king over them."[15] Did Israel have a king? Yes. Absolutely. God was their absolute leader and authority during the entire time of the judges. So, the story of Judges is not about how Israel did not have the right political leader or ideology, *but what happens when human beings reject the absolute authority of the one true King.*[16]

When humans lower their eyes from God to *self*. When humans elevate themselves to the top of the evolutionary food chain. When self is elevated above all else, people are left to do what is right in their own eyes. A brilliant stroke from the writer of Judges.

When people reject the true King, they do what is right in their own minds because they have no one and nothing to lift their eyes to. Nothing to focus on or derive broader existential meaning from and no one to say what's right or wrong. We have no way to console ourselves because we cannot contrive our own value simply from within ourselves. We can't just muster up enough to be enough. We stand absolutely alone. Living in our tiny home left to spend hours scrolling.

Contriving.
Comparing.
Controlling.

Leading to dramatic consequences for how humans are to be in the world as Adam and Eve's eyes were not just opened; they had a completely new perspective on the world. What they were told would bring death is now seen as "a delight to the eyes." What was once seen as vice is now seen as virtue, accepted as gospel and not merely accepted but lauded from rooftops and fully embraced with open arms as something that would make "one wise." What a world. We don't know anything about this as modern people where vice would become virtue or where truth would become heresy. A world where there are no taboos and nothing off limits as to what humans want to make of themselves.

A world known for....
....self-expression.
....deconstruction.
....autonomy.

The creation exchanging themselves for the Creator. Oh wait....this sounds a lot like where we are in our cultural moment (or at the very least an accurate depiction of Twitter).

I don't mean to say we all started with evil

intentions to curse God. Notice again how the serpent made his initial appeal as he said to our ancestors: "you will be like God, knowing good and evil." The appeal was that they would "be like God" and become like God. *The deepest temptation here is actually not to some sort of vice, but to virtue.* The serpent is actually trying to tug on Adam and Eve's good desires to get them into sin. He was saying, "No, no, no Eve….you're missing the point here. God just has better things for you ahead. What He really knows is that when you eat it, you will be like Him." He is spinning the very truths of God to sound kingdom-esque but, as we will find out, are completely devoid of the one true King.

Offering the kingdom without the King.[17]

An offer that was first and foremost brought in the form of a new narrative. Remember God's narrative about the tree was, "Don't eat it, you will die." Yet the serpent's narrative was "eat it, you will *not* die." Chiefly, this is a matter of competing narratives about what brings life and death. The initial issue at work was not framed as a matter of breaking laws but as a new narrative. Meaning that the first work of humans is to understand the story we are currently inhabiting and recalibrate ourselves to God's narrative about what truly brings flourishing and life.

Unfortunately, Adam and Eve fell for the narrative of the serpent leading to a sudden realization. After the exchange between the serpent and our ancestors we are told, "then the eyes of both were opened, and they knew that they were naked." Previously "the man and his wife were both naked and were not ashamed"[18] but now there is a dramatic shift taking place. A shift that is seen in a wordplay in Hebrew, as the crafty (*arum*) serpent, led Adam and Eve to the awareness that they are naked (*arumim*). Through the lies of the crafty serpent, humans had become crafty as well. Therefore leading to the sudden realization of their own nakedness and a focus exclusively on self.[19]

A focus that led humans to cover themselves for the first time. Upon realizing they were naked, "they sewed fig leaves together and made themselves loincloths." Fully aware of their own nakedness, they attempt to cover up in shame by making themselves "loincloths." Before this, God made everything the people needed. Now, we see humans attempting to cover up in their own self-sufficiency and create their own covering.

The first result when humans elevate self is to manufacture their own identity. Cultural commentator, Alan Noble, writes to this end: "At the heart of the secular age is the individual in their effort to create and project an identity in a chaotic age and hostile world."[20] When one's eyes are truly opened and self becomes king, humans are left striving to create, construct and project an identity in the chaos of our age. Left to post about how "Everything is Awesome" yet so utterly out of control. Stuck in a never ending hamster wheel as we are instantly bombarded with Edenic-like identity projections.

Be like Jocko and wake up at 3:59 AM.
Find a relationship like Colton and Cassie.
Have the perfect family like the Bucket List Family.

Do more.
Be better.
Work harder.

Yet in this hamster wheel of identity projection,

we make an attempt to create something that God never intended us to have. A self-made construct that flies in the face of our Creator *as our identity is something we work from, not for.* It is something freely given, bestowed from our Creator since the very beginning. But without the Creator, we are left to our own devices. Spending our entire lives striving to keep up the identity that we created and constructed, leading to the total inability to just be. [21] Stuck in our tiny home late at night, *scrolling*. Unable to focus our *eyes*.

§

Where do we even go from here? I did warn you that this was going to get really dark. My goal in writing this is not to make you feel utterly hopeless but to identify the core *problem* at work. We all know that everyone has an opinion about what the real problem is (if you don't believe me, just go watch *Fox News* + *CNN* on the same evening and see how disorienting our times are).

All too often our presupposition is to go to modern solutions because we think we are dealing with modern problems but our approaches do not even begin to scratch the surface of what it truly means to be human. Stuff like bamboo straws and moving into tiny homes are merely modern attempts at ancient, deeply human problems (sorry, my minimalist friends. Seriously, I've got nothing personally against you).

When we get to the core of this deep, human problem, it opens the potential for the solution for our souls. A timeless solution in every space and place that lifts our eyes from being solely focused on immanent realities to a transcedant narrative about the one true King. Even as we continue to struggle to stop scrolling and get past self, a *person* meets us where we're at. The Creator pursues the creation with an *invitation*. Or, as we will find out in the next chapter, a *Father* who is walking.

Part Two:

The Invitation

Father

"Come to daddy."

An invitation I gave my son when he hid for the first time. Like, we are talking the first time ever he hid in my presence. This was pre playing hide-and-seek for hours on end while my son hides in the same spot for the hundredth time (and *every* time it's just as much as a surprise to him that I found him). It was a strange moment, that felt like time slowed down.

The strangest part was that I have no idea how we got there. I was just doing some dishes as a part of my normal routine (one of my favorite pastimes as the official dish washer in my family - a role that I am forever destined to fulfill since I have *zero* cooking abilities). All I heard was Ephraim scream and the pitter patter of his little legs working as hard as possible to run away from whatever he had sensed he had done wrong.

As I heard Ephraim scream and run away, I ran as fast as possible into the other room to figure out what had happened. As I walked in, all I saw was little E hiding in the corner of our living room with his face buried into the wall. Gently I called out, "Ephraim," to no avail or response. For some reason, he refused to turn around and his face continued to be firmly planted in the corner of the room (again, I have no idea why he hid. He didn't even wake me up at 3:59 AM that day).

I walked towards him slowly but surely until I was a few feet away. Again, I gently and tenderly called out, "Ephraim." This time he slowly looked over his shoulder but then in an instant buried his head back into the corner.

Eventually, I crouched down to Ephraim's height and simply said, "Ephraim, it's okay....come here buddy." From this invitation little E turned around, revealing a picture that will forever be etched on my mind. All I could see on his face was the look of *shame*.

I couldn't believe it. I was at a complete loss for words. I was seeing my son experience shame for the first time. It wasn't even something I taught him. He felt shame so naturally as his first instinct was to hide himself.

Not to talk it out.
Not to seek out help.
Not to come to his daddy.

Finally, I crouched down to his level and spread my arms as wide as possible. Then, I whispered one of the most powerful statements in the entire world:

"Ephraim, *daddy* is here."

Daddy. A word that creates worlds. A word that echoes throughout the created order. A word that has been called upon in every tribe and tongue.

Ephraim took it all in for a moment, and I could see the gears spinning in his head as he processed his next move in light of my bold declaration. A declaration that fundamentally changed everything as he ran into my wide open arms and I got to wipe away his tears, whispering to him how it would all be okay and that nothing could separate him from my love because I am and forever will be his *father*.

Yeah, father. I know. Talk about a loaded word.

Infused with memories of years of care....or lots of counseling (can I get an amen, all my counseling peeps?). A word that conjures up images of tenderness or trauma. A word that can be unforgettable at times. A word that we all can understand.

Well, understand may be the wrong word. We can all understand "father" in a biological sense (if you don't get how it all works, I can explain it to you when you're older). But there's a good chance we never really grasp it in a relational sense.

(* Now we're getting to the deep end of the pool folks. Pool may be the wrong word if your father was twisted and demented like mine, believing wholeheartedly in the "push you into the deep end and watch you drown" approach to child-rearing. Let's just say my counselor and I have got a few more years of work to do)

For many of us, "father" is a loaded term, especially when it pertains to God.[1] 20th century pastor and theologian, J.B. Phillips, unpacks this in his short but jam-packed book, *Your God is Too Small*. He writes about what he calls the "parental hangover," as "the early conception of God is almost invariably founded upon the child's idea of his (or her)[2] Father....if the child is afraid (or, worse still, afraid and feeling guilty because he is afraid) of his father, the chances are that his Father in Heaven will appear to him a fearful Being."[3] For better or worse, our understanding of father (and God as Father) is inextricably tied to our childhoods, making the term quite loaded and explosive.

Now this does not mean that we are forever doomed by the image of the father of our youth. It's not like Jesus in His original context did not understand that the people He taught had some real baggage when it came to their earthly fathers. He fully understood humanity's often tense relationships with their earthly fathers and how everyone's got some form of daddy issues. So much so that He *still* chose to use this metaphor as the predominant one for God. Phillips writes:

> Christ Himself taught us to regard God as Father. Are we to reject His own analogy? Of course not, so long as we remember that it is an analogy. When Christ taught His disciples to regard God as their Father in Heaven He

did not mean that their idea of God must necessarily be based upon their ideas of their own fathers. For all we know there may have been (*definitely was....*)[4] many of His hearers whose fathers were unjust, tyrannical, stupid, conceited, feckless, or indulgent. It is the relationship that Christ is stressing. The intimate love for, and interest in, his son possessed by a good earthly father represents to men (and women)[5] a relationship that they can understand, even if themselves are fatherless![6]

Jesus' use of Father is not fundamentally tied to our earthly fathers at all. Jesus was fully aware of his followers' issues yet knew that this analogy was *exactly* what their souls needed. He knew that his listeners would have conceptions of father that were ill-informed, deeply scarring and that may take years to undo. With this understanding, Jesus still knew that humans deepest need was not to run from false conceptions of father but run to a more robust, truer picture of what father really means based on the template of our Father in Heaven.[7]

That all earthly fathers were mere shadows to

the one true Father. *A Father* who has pursued us since the very beginning of time. *A Father* who refuses to let go until the dire end and would sacrifice anything for His own. *A Father* who is compassionate, gracious and slow to anger.[8] *A Father* who came on the scene in a garden called Eden.

§

Genesis 3:8-15 // And they heard the sound of the Lord God walking in the garden in the cool of the day, and the man and his wife hid themselves from the presence of the Lord God among the trees of the garden. But the Lord God called to the man and said to him, "Where are you?" And he said, "I heard the sound of you in the garden, and I was afraid, because I was naked, and I hid myself." He said, "Who told you that you were naked? Have you eaten of the tree of which I commanded you not to eat?" The man said, "The woman whom you gave to be with me, she gave me fruit of the tree, and I ate." Then the Lord God said to the woman, "What is this that

you have done?" The woman said, "The
serpent deceived me, and I ate."

The Lord God said to the serpent,
"Because you have done this,
    cursed are you above all livestock
    and above all beasts of the field;
on your belly you shall go,
    and dust you shall eat
    all the days of your life.
I will put enmity between you and the
woman,
    and between your offspring and her
offspring;
he shall bruise your head,
    and you shall bruise his heel."

Immediately after Adam and Eve's eyes had been
opened, we are told about how God is *walking*.
Genesis 3:8 tells us, "And they heard the sound of
the Lord God walking in the garden in the cool
of the day." The granddaddy sin that started all
sins just took place. The pinnacle of God's creation
had turned away, lowered their eyes solely on self,
violating the only sacred prohibition, and ushering
in total shame and brokenness into the world. Yet

in the midst of this, God is going for a nice stroll in the cool of the day. Not in a hurry. Nowhere to be. iPhone left charging at home. Just walking.

Strange.
Startling.
Suspicious.

What if those texting bubbles finally turned into an actual text? (* Sorry to remind you, my *super* single friend. Look - if they don't respond, they weren't right for you anyways).

As God comes walking on the scene, notice His name. This isn't just the "CEO" God strolling on the scene, but "the Lord God." *Yahweh Elohim*, the personal name for God, is being used. The serpent sold our ancestors on the lie that God was merely some distant deity and not deeply personal. More so the big vision "CEO" or an impersonal energy force than the person next to us in the intricate workings of our world. Yet even in the midst of great sin and tragedy, God is still personally walking onto the scene.

He is present.

He is personal.
He is pursuing.

Like another day in Eden, it's business as usual as God desires to be with His people. To meet them in their deep wounds. To commune with His creation. To just be with them.

Yet we all know that though God wanted to be, humans had fundamentally changed. This is clearly evident as Adam and Eve "hid themselves from the presence of the Lord God." The personal Creator goes for a stroll to commune with His creation, but His creation is nowhere to be found. Stood up on a date in the cool of the day.

To make matters worse, they do not just hide; notice where they hide. Adam and Eve hide "among the trees of the garden." They are hiding among the very provision that "the Lord God made to spring up.... that is pleasant to the sight."[9] *The trees that God had made for His creation to gaze at are now the very hiding place to prevent God from seeing them.* A tragic reversal. A cosmic game of hide-and-seek gone terribly wrong, leading to separation and distance between the Creator and His creation.

But what would God do in response to His people hiding? Unleash His holy vindictive wrath and come down with the hammer like the vengeful Father many think Him to be? Our all too common expectation can be similar to that of the theologian Jim Carrey in *Bruce Almighty*, as he declares to the heavens "Smite Me, O Mighty Smiter!"

Bring it! Strike me down! Break down the door and tell me everything I have ever done wrong because I know You're keeping track up there in Your holy abode! And then we wait. Waiting for that holy lightning bolt to strike so all can see who God *really* is.

A God who is petty.
A God who is pissed off.
A God who is the divine punisher.
A God who wakes us up at 3:59 AM and turns on all the lights (or maybe that's just my kids).

Yet as we wait for God's vindictive response from the heavens, nothing happens. We feel shame. We feel self-condemnation. We feel that there should be some sort of consequences. Maybe a slap on the wrist so we know He's actually paying attention? At this point, we would even take the texting bubbles popping up with no response and the texting receipt "seen at 3:59 AM" as we would know He at least read what we sent (why did anyone ever think that was a good idea?). Yet still no God. Maybe He's taking a stroll? Still walking, with no iPhone.

But eventually, God does show up to respond - but not in the way we expect. We are told, "but the Lord God called to the man and said to him, 'Where are you?'"

No divine gavel?
No thunder and lighting?
No fog machine like my local megachurch?
Just the Lord God, simply coming to ask a question.

But do you think God knew where they were? Do you think the all-knowing, ever-present, all-powerful, sovereign King of the universe who created the very fabric of this world's existence by merely speaking could figure out where His only two human creations were? Gently but assuredly nod your head yes. He totally knew where they were, and *in His question we find His character*.

God patiently and personally comes on the scene, not with accusation but rather a question. *He doesn't come as a preacher bellowing judgement but as a counselor inviting confession.* The great Counselor of our souls who meets us in our despair over our brokenness and the brokenness of the world. An ever-present, loving Father whose deepest desire is for His kids to come back to Him as a Father who wants it all.

Our deepest fears.
Our deepest shame.
Our deepest anxieties.

To be brought directly to Him so He can bring healing and hope to the deep places of shame in our lives and world. To be clear, I know this can be disorienting. I'm with you. But it is imperative we learn to let God speak for Himself as all too often:

We let the media and political agendas define our template for God.
We let an angry and abusive earthly father become our template for God.
We let vague and abstract systematic theology books set our template for God.

Yet none of these are God. Or better said, none of these are "the Lord God." Maybe the Lord God can speak for Himself? Maybe He has and is speaking but we're not listening? The personal presence of God walking.

Ready to listen.
Ready to commune.
Ready to ask that question.

Where are you?

A holy invitation for the creation to be with their Creator. What an idea. Maybe *the* idea of all ideas. To be....with God. What a concept. It can't be that simple.

Well, if this is the point of our creation, how are we to respond to God walking on the scene? Maybe our ancestors can prepare us for being with our Father and not making this whole thing about self? Just maybe. To God's unlikely question, Adam responds, "I heard the sound of you in the garden, and I was afraid, because I was naked, and I hid myself." Simple. Straight-forward. Yet highly redacted.

See, Adam's order of events begins with God walking but he casually leaves out the whole thing about a talking snake, the Parseltongue convo Eve had and the eating of the fruit that marred all of creation (how do you forget that?). Adam had been watching the news on his TV and noticed that "good" news always takes creative liberties. His response is "based on a true story," but not exactly the order of events itself (sort of like how Denzel is going to play me in the movie about my life). Minor tweaks. 2 degrees type of stuff. The sort of stuff that fundamentally changes the narrative.

Adam makes the issue about God walking instead of any sort of personal responsibility for what he and Eve had done. The morning news headline the next day in Eden – "God, On the Wrong Side of History." Gosh, I thought that whole God is dead quote was bad for PR, but now this? Ugh. Maybe God needs to go on Oprah or Ellen to make a statement because the Twitter apology just didn't do it. Now there are death threats as well and He's put on trial via Twitter to be hung in the court of public opinion. No real facts. But plenty of feelings.

Ah, yes, so many feelings. Adam was quick to point

out how he felt in this circumstance. He pointed out that the second he heard God walking, that he was "afraid." Case closed. Adam shared his feelings in a long post on Facebook, so it must be true. God, that vindictive, cruel, speed walking Father. Just barging in with no consideration for one's privacy. He could have at least texted beforehand. A DM, at least?

How cruel.
How judgy.
How subjective.

I'm not saying feelings don't matter or that emotional intelligence is not a vital part of our health and wholeness, but our feelings are not objective truth. They are merely subjective and it would be wise for us to form a natural skepticism towards our own feelings as they are only the tip of the iceberg revealing something existentially deeper....*our identity*.

Adam and Eve had developed a self-constructed identity. Adam tells God that he did all of this "because I was naked." This is key as this is Adam's identity statement. Before the Fall, he and Eve "were both naked and were not ashamed."[10]

No fear.

No shame.

No covering.

Totally lost in, awoken and enamored by the very presence of their Father. But upon transgressing God's directive, *they became consumed with an identity based in self and the lies of the serpent.* [11] An identity leading the creation to now boldly proclaim to the Creator, "You don't understand, God. This is just the way I am. I was born this way. You made me this way!" Confusing. Shame-filled. Chock full of self-professed, feeling-filled, subjective identity markers.

But again, why would God say vice is now virtue? He must be confused, or at the very least thoroughly inconsistent. Maybe this whole dialogue is a grand adventure in missing the point and missing the key issue at play in our own identity statements that we proclaim to God.

The key issue in our age of identity confusion is not about God but that we have lowered our eyes from our true Father and His divine truth, making self the lowest common denominator. [12] That's

what Adam does when he tells God, "I hid myself."
Adam's solution to the problem of his shame is
solely based in self and what he could make happen.
This whole thing is now all about Adam and him
discovering himself. If only God never went walking
in the first place.

So, the formula:
Blame God.
Base reasoning entirely in subjective feelings.
Embrace a new identity rooted in sin.
Make the whole thing about self.

I think I've seen this one before. What if Adam had
taken responsibility for his sin (or at least issued a
half-baked Twitter apology)? Notice Adam never
says, "I did this and it was wrong." He makes it
about God, shares his feelings, proudly proclaims
his new identity and makes it about himself. But, he
never takes personal responsibility for the mess he
and Eve are in.

I don't want to speculate, but I always wonder what
would have happened if Adam and Eve merely
took ownership (or extreme ownership....thanks
Jocko. Hoo-rah!). I can't help but imagine that

this narrative would have gone in a very different direction. Maybe God would have invited them to go walking with Him? Yet at this point, I want to be careful of over speculation because this brilliant author has given us this narrative for a reason.

In this narrative, the first place God goes after is Adam's identity statement. He simply responds to our ancestors (again with a question), "Who told you that you were naked?" *Who told you that you were naked?* Straight for the jugular. Or, better said, straight for the identity statement about who Adam thought he was, not who he was created to be. Isn't this what God does? He doesn't just focus on what we do, but who we are. The realities that hover below the surface of our lives, becoming *the* fundamental narratives that we live unless someone like the Father gently comes to remind us of who we were really created to be.

The narratives that are the first place our true Father meets us. Narratives that when addressed make meaningful and lasting change *as from our identity stems our actions.* This is why the second question (not the first) is, "Have you eaten of the tree of which I commanded you not to eat?" God does address our actions, but first He wants to root out the self-proclaimed identity that is creating the actions in the first place. He desires to create long-lasting, meaningful change. Not just a picture or status change on social media, but meaningful change that gets to the core of our humanity. That roots out all of the rivals competing for our eyes in our attention economy and that calls us home from the chaos to just be with our Father.

The type of change that only comes from a God who is willing to ask questions. Notice God has yet to make a declarative statement in our story. He just asks questions which are the very means to how God brings His people to the place of self-awareness.

A God who is….
….patient.
….present.
….walking.

Maybe this would lead Adam and Eve to finally figure it out, but I think at this point we all have a pessimistic streak growing towards humanity. Our ancestors' response continues to show humans' inability to just be as they pivot to blaming-shifting. Adam answers God's questions by saying, "The woman whom you gave to be with me, she gave me fruit of the tree, and I ate." Immediately, Adam blames the woman for his sin. Adam does what is the plight of our age, blaming someone else (most likely trashing them on a burner Twitter account).

It's also much deeper than that. *He isn't just blaming his covenant partner, but also his Creator.* He said it was "the woman *you* gave to me." Adam is blaming God for even giving him Eve in the first place, trying to justify what he did by the circumstance God put him in and by playing the victim card. Declaring, "You should feel bad for me because You don't understand what she's like to live with. Please, God, send me another because You created this very mess."

You.
You.
You.

A response thoroughly rooted in self and a fundamental misunderstanding of the Father. The creation blaming the Creator. What a scene.

Maybe Eve would fare better with God's question. We see God engaging Eve when, "the Lord God said to the woman, "What is this that you have done? The woman said, "The serpent deceived me, and I ate." Eve does a little better than Adam. She mentions speaking in Parseltongue and the whole serpent thing so she's trending in the right direction. Now, she's more like *NPR* than *CNN* or *Fox News* (or more like Channing Tatum playing me in the movie of my life). A little less bias, just stating the facts.

But is this what God was *really* asking for? Remember, back to that whole God knows everything we've ever done and is everywhere all at once. Eve is right in one sense as the serpent did deceive her, but still no one is taking personal responsibility for what has happened. Ultimately, she is just a more subtle version of Adam playing the victim card to her Father. Still making it about self and focusing on feelings as the grand arbiter of truth versus receiving the Father's invitation to go walking.

How would God clean up this complete mess and utter catastrophe? Smite His creation as we pondered earlier or do something starkly different? You're probably picking up at this point that it's the latter.

Notice who God speaks to first in the midst of human sin, autonomy and self-exaltation. We are told, "The Lord God said to the serpent." God speaks directly to that crafty serpent. What in the world? I'm not God but at this point I think we would all say it's fair for God to let the thunder bolts roll down because there needs to be consequences for humans. *Yet God first goes for the serpent, not the sinner.* God is going for the very root of evil in our world. The dark spiritual force at work behind the curtain of human history. Dealing with Supreme Leader Snoke, not just some First Order destroyers. Dealing with the Mind Flyer, not just the Demogorgon. Fundamentally, *God is getting to the root of evil, not merely the fruit.*

As God deals with the root of all evil, He is incredibly intentional with His wording around curses. He only curses two realities in this account: 1) the serpent and 2) the ground.[13] He does not curse humans. Yes, He unquestionably corrects humans through dramatic ramifications on the basic human institutions of child-rearing, marriage and work, but He does not curse humans. *In the subtle distinction between curses and correction we find an important facet of God's character.*

This distinction comes down to the fundamental difference between guilt and shame. Fundamentally, guilt addresses *what we've done* while shame addresses *who we are*. Guilt is about *action* while shame is about *identity*. You should feel guilty when you do something wrong or you're probably just a complete sociopath (sorry, a little bleak again). Guilt is a necessity for anyone who is not named Ted Bundy or Charles Manson and is a powerful motivator for human change. But shame gets deeper as it speaks to one's core identity. Modern day millennial patron saint, Brene Brown, speaks to this (in a Ted Talk, of course): "Shame is a focus on self, guilt is a focus on behavior. Shame is, 'I am bad.' Guilt is, 'I did something bad.'"[14] Shame is focused on *self*.

Brilliant. Now we know Adam and Eve's problem. In their shame, they became evermore rooted in an ideology of self. But God in His grace, tries to lift His people's eyes to their true Father. And as their true Father, He does correct His kids but does not curse or shame them. *Even in God's correction, we find His character.*

God even goes as far as blessing in the middle of cursing. As God first speaks directly to the serpent He proclaims, "I will put enmity between you and the woman, and between your offspring and her offspring; he shall bruise your head, and you shall bruise his heel." God is speaking of two parties who will experience great hostility between one another. A tension that will fundamentally come between the offspring of the serpent and the offspring of the woman (Eve).

A generational tension that will continue on into the future, but there will be a day where "He," a single future offspring of Eve will "bruise" the head of the serpent. To be clear, we are not just talking about a slight discoloration under the skin; "bruise" is the word for "crush" or "strike" in Hebrew. It is an aggressive war term that means that the future seed of Eve will kill the serpent. Yet the serpent will also do substantial damage to this future offspring of Eve in fatally wounding this one in an epic struggle of good versus evil.

I don't want to jump too far ahead in the biblical story yet, but this becomes the very tension throughout the rest of the scriptures through the coming of Jesus. Later biblical authors see Jesus as the fulfillment of the offspring of Eve who crushed the serpent's head, but in the process was fatally injured on the cross.[15] Many theologians believe this text in Genesis is the first preaching of the Gospel in the entirety of scripture. Even in the midst of curses, God blesses all of humanity with future promises of His restoration and renewal that will ring throughout the cosmos. *God declares hope in the ashes and beauty in the brokenness.* A Father whose first action is to roll out His cosmic redemptive plan for His creation.

(* Sidenote - Where do you think J.K. Rowling got her entire plot? Harry dies yet kills Voldomort in the process and then Harry resurrects again. *Harry Potter* is basically the Gospel story....).

Finally, as God rolls out His promises, He also protects his people. Right after God speaks these curses and corrections, "the Lord God made for Adam and for his wife garments of skins and clothed them."[16] The Lord God gives Adam and Eve matching parkas as He knows the long journey they have set out on due to the new identity and actions they chose. Actions that have real ramifications and caused our ancestors to wander far from home into a deeper spiral of sin and self-destruction. *Yet even in correction, God covers His people.*

He guards.
He shields.
He protects.

He leads with compassion and care for His creation to a people who clearly don't deserve it, demonstrating a mark of pure, unfiltered grace. By now we should see this ever emerging picture of who God *actually* is.

A God who....
....loves walking.
....asks questions.
....brings consolation.
....covers when He corrects.
....always operates according to His character.

Yet we also see humans who....

....constantly scroll.

....lower their eyes.

....play the victim card.

....regularly struggle to just be.

A strange partnership as the Creator is insistent on not giving up on His creation. The Creator, or better said, the true *Father*. Who desires nothing but going *walking* with his kids.

§

Again, I know this is not always the conception of the *person* of the Father that we automatically think of. All too often we read Genesis 3 and only see a vindictive, cruel Creator smiting His creation for just eating a piece of fruit. But this narrative really reveals how even when humanity continues to spiral deeper into the same issues, God's character is thoroughly consistent through it all.

A gracious, loving Father coming with an *invitation* to His kids in the midst of their deep shame. A narrative display that this chapter is not primarily about how "God and humans can no longer converse, but rather the difficulty that the human heart and mind can have in genuinely trusting God as a wise creator."[17] Or better said, the difficulty that humans have in trusting God as Father.

This is a narrative that I have sat with for years (since that whole losing my first love thing) that has literally helped me rebuild my entire framework of who God is and even more so, who I am. A narrative that is central to our theology (thoughts about God) and our anthropology (thoughts about humanity). A narrative manifesto boldly declaring to the world who our Father is and who we are to become in the process as His kids. The inevitable rub off between a Father and His kids who just spend time being with one another.

This true and full understanding of this person in the Father leads us to the *purpose* of our entire existence. The very fabric of why we were created and the end to which we were created is simply demonstrated through reorienting our lives to the Father. Or, as we will explore in the next chapter, the *telos* for which we were created all along.

Chapter 4

Telos

Why? The question of all questions. The question that starts every existential crisis (as well as every backpacking trip through Europe).

The very question Facebook employees were asking as they walked into the office on January 30th, 2019.[1] An auspicious Wednesday morning as many employees of Facebook found that they could not accomplish their most rudimentary tasks. Calendar apps were not working. Digital bus schedules were completely offline. Cafeteria menus were not updating. Local games of Words with Friends were tragically put on hold (no idea if this last part was true, but just imagine the sheer chaos).

This catastrophe came at the hands of tech rival Apple shutting down all of Facebook's apps. I know this seems improbable based on the evil empire that is Facebook, but it did actually happen (and Steve Jobs definitely laughed from the grave).

See, all of the tasks that Facebook employees tried to accomplish all took place on apps built by

Facebook. Yet Facebook had violated a number of Apple's privacy policies by stealing user data, so Apple shut all their apps down. Now, you may wonder how it's possible for Apple to shut down all of the apps for Facebook's 35,000 employees. It arises from the fundamental difference between an app and an operating system (I am a pastor so this explanation is about to be really simple. The following explanation is also for all who understood my reference to a "TV").

Essentially, Facebook is an app. It is something you go to the app store and download for your various devices. There are millions of apps you can download, and we use all sorts of apps for all aspects of our lives. We've got apps for everything from tracking our personal finances, health and fitness progress (especially our daily step minimums), listening to podcasts and books, and planning every part of our day-to-day lives. Apps are central to the operation of our lives (and it seriously took me *years* to use the calendars app. Now I only have like 3 paper planners and the rest are digital).

Whatever the app may be from the myriad of options, all apps have to request access from an operating system to use their platform. So, when you're trying to capture that pristine selfie that you climbed to the top of Kilimanjaro to get, your social media platform (like Facebook) has to request access to use the camera from your operating system (I know you hiked just for the selfie. No one will believe it happened if it's not on social media). Or when an app wants to use your data it has to request permission from the operating system to get access to your information (hence why Facebook was and is in deep trouble). Overall, the real power is in the operating system.

The most common operating systems are in our pockets at all times through things like Android or iOS (the iPhone). Operating systems are central to how our technology runs and operates on a day-to-day basis. They are the foundation for everything you see and interact with on your phone, behaving like the brain does to the rest of the body as it controls everything that happens on our devices. Hence, why Apple was able to shut all of Facebook down in one fatal blow and why operating systems are where the money is at.

The great irony is that most people want to focus

on inventing some cool app versus seeing the bigger picture in an operating system. Similarly, this is how we treat our personal growth and spiritual lives. It's hip to focus on finding one life hack to instantly change our lives versus spending intentional time focusing on the entire operating system that governs all of our core decisions. Spending all of our time consumed with trying to find the how yet never considering the deeper *why*.

In many ways, this has been reflective in the numerous studies on how we change as humans. Fields like modern neuroscience and habit formation have added much to our understanding of how we change. One of the most basic and remarkable truths from the field of neuroscience is "that the power to direct our attention has within it the power to shape our brain's firing patterns, as well as the power to shape the architecture of the brain itself."[2] We have the power to fundamentally *change the architecture of our brain* through intentional focus.

Come on - what a super power! Who wants to be an Avenger when we have the ability to change our brains? Actually, I would still take being T'Challa for a day (RIP Chadwick Boseman, and of course....Wakanda Forever!). But if that were not an option, a close second is being able to change the architecture of my brain.

This can be accomplished through mechanisms like the "habit loop." This is a mechanism where "you must *decide* to change {insert habit you want to change here}. You must consciously accept the hard work of identifying the cues and rewards that drive the habit's routines, and find alternatives."[3] You are a few life hacks away from redesigning the hundreds of habits that govern your daily life. Time to Marie Kondo your life, move into a tiny home and join your local Crossfit gym. Whatever you want, you can just go and do it once you figure out the basic habits that govern your life.

These concepts not only apply to habits but also to the cultivation of vocational skills and a craft.[4] If you look up research on how world-class experts become world-class experts (in any field), you will find the "ten-thousand hour rule" popularized by Malcolm Gladwell. It takes "ten thousand hours of practice....to achieve the level of mastery associated with being a world-class expert—in anything."[5] Like, anything. You can go and do it, so go and do it. In 10,000 hours, you can become a world class chess player, boomerang thrower or crossfitter. So what are you waiting for? Go get after it. Be the change you want to see in the world. The end.

What a book, right? Surprising twist based on the previous three chapters and humanity's total inability to follow through. There must be more to the story than mere human ability to do?

I definitely need to add a *but*. There is always a but. Buts rarely make best sellers though.

You Are a Badass….BUT.
Think and Grow Rich….BUT.
The Obstacle is the Way….BUT.

The titles just don't have the same ring to them, yet adding but is profoundly human and it's way more honest on how life actually works for us normal folk (yes, these are real titles….not the *but* part of course).

A modern understanding of how we change can profoundly aid our lives, but it is not enough to actually change it for the long haul. In neuroscience, for example, "neuroplasticity can be either a helper or a hindrance, depending on how you are unconsciously choosing to act and focus your attention."[6] Neuroplasticity is not inherently making an ethical or moral claim on what actions are good or bad. It is not contending for the type of person you should become (or if you should go on that backpacking trip through Europe. Yes, you should go, but that's beside the point). Neuroplasticity is a neurological process for how we grow through intentional practice. But *why* should we grow into any given goal and *what* are we actually supposed to be formed into (like what or who is our model for growth)?

For example, think about the "new year, new you" type of stuff (which I EAT UP, of course). This type A, Enneagram 3, (recovering) performer lives and breathes for goals and mountains to climb (figurative, of course; I hate hiking. Sorry, Pacific Northwest. It's not you, it's me). But, as I plan my year, how should I decide what mountain I'm going to climb? How do I know which goals are merely arbitrary constructions and which have actual depth and meaning? Because I would guess you're a lot like me.

You crave purpose.

You crave deeper meaning.

You crave something to give your life to.

Neuroscience, habit formation or any of the self-proclaimed self-help gurus of our day cannot make a definitive statement about why you should do anything at all or even make an objective claim on what you should shoot for as the goal of your growth. Therein lies the deep seated anxiety and confusion of our age.

We desire answers to the deep existential questions that no amount of studies in neuroscience, habits or self-improvement can ever provide. This is the stuff of Plato, Aristotle, or may I dare say….Jesus. This is the stuff of philosophy and theology, not merely self-help (which is usually no-help, by the way). We need a better and deeper why for our growth and development or we will continue to live our lives as existential toddlers in the shallow end of the pool.

Ancient Greek philosophers spoke to this with the idea of a "telos." They would spend their days philosophizing about the meaning of life (basically, it's what my hipster friends and I do over our morning salted cream cold foam cold brew....can't do the guji every day, got to switch it up). As these Greek philosophers philosophized, they would spend their lives debating the telos of humanity. Questions like:

What is the good life?
What is the end to which we are created?
What is our ultimate aim or goal as human beings?

These questions are at the core of what each of us must answer because they are the very ends that will become our magnetic north and calibrate our hearts to live a life of deep meaning and purpose.[7] These questions have the making of not merely a career but a calling that we can give our lives to. These questions are the very questions that get deep into our bones and fill us every morning with purpose, meaning and *hope*.

Hope.

A word that we desperately need today (and one I do still believe in despite my ever-growing cynicism towards humanity). A belief that our lives are not made by mere happenstance but by a good and loving Father who is the actual end to which we were created. Everything else merely serves as a means to this end.

Whether we realize it or not, we are implicitly living our lives with some sort of telos as we speak.[8] Like, this very millisecond our most rudimentary habits are leading us to some end that is what we are giving our lives for. For example a common telos of our age is found in the American Dream. Get a steady paycheck, get married, have babies, build a white picket fence, retirement and death. But this is probably not your template if you're drinking the guji.

Probably more so something like this: Move from job-to-job trying to find your "passion." Go on that backpacking trip we talked about. Get into a relationship. Another backpacking trip and/or vision quest. Live with your girlfriend or boyfriend to test the waters. Master's degree because the job market sucks. Eventually decide to make it official after 7 years of dating. Build your career, two incomes. Have a kid, really late (you're finally ready after having a dog together for the last 7 years). Then settle in. Suburbs, retirement, death.

We did it. What a life that leads all of us to the same place. In a nice rocking chair in some awful retirement community with horrible sweet potatoes. And as we sit in that crappy rocking chair, we will have a sudden realization of the telos of our lives. The end you lived and gave everything for. *A moment that will either bring great pride or panic as we realize whether we lived for the end or merely a means to an end.* If we lived our lives moving from a myriad of hows (and how-tos) or with an actual why.

But what if we could figure out our why now? What if we didn't have to wait for those horrible sweet potatoes? What if we could discover early on in our lives the true telos which we were created for since the very beginning?

The telos that can get us through every trial and temptation. *The telos* that can propel us through the deepest of valleys and the highest of mountains (especially to help us get that selfie). *The telos* that will go darn well with those retirement home sweet potatoes. *The telos* that leads us to a garden called Eden.

§

Genesis 3:22-24 // Then the Lord God said, "Behold, the man has become like one of us in knowing good and evil. Now, lest he reach out his hand and take also of the tree of life and eat, and live forever—" therefore the Lord God sent him out from the garden of Eden to work the ground from which he was taken. He drove out the man, and at the east of the garden of Eden he placed the cherubim and a flaming sword that turned every way to guard the way to the tree of life.

Humans, in their attempt at self-sufficiency, had *become* something. Right after God covered His people by His own character, we are told "Then the Lord God said, "Behold, the man has become...." Clearly the Creator's character hadn't changed, but His creation had as they had become something.

Earlier in Genesis 2, we see the same word become used in a very different sense. When God formed the man and breathed the breath of life into him, we were told he "became a living creature."[9] When God created the woman and bonded Adam and Eve in the covenant of marriage we were told, "and they shall become one flesh."[10] Every time before this moment in Genesis 3, becoming was used in a positive way yet here we see a new narrative emerging.

A new narrative of how our ancestors had become like God through their epic fail. God says in the story, "Behold, the man has become like one of us in knowing good and evil." It becomes evident from God Himself that humanity had become like Him. Out of all the things God could have said in the wake of the Fall, that doesn't sound too bad. Actually, that sounds pretty darn good (go humans, we did it! First point on the board for the human race). Maybe that's the point or telos of this whole thing?

To *become* like God.

Doing God-type stuff like:
Using bamboo straws.
Moving to a tiny home.
Tweeting against injustice.
Recycling kombucha bottles.
Why not #FeeltheBern while we're at it.
Become like God (or at least *our* picture of God).

But may I dare say, what if we have it backwards? What if becoming like God isn't actually the first step? Notice after humans had become like their Creator, God says, "Now, lest he reach out his hand and take also of the tree of life and eat, and live forever." It is evident that God is chiefly concerned about a tree. *The* tree of life that we know to be in the very center of the garden of Eden itself as the very place where all life would flow from for humans. Yet this tree did not merely have some "magical" power within itself as the tree of life's power came from its proximity to the author of life, the Lord God, at the center of the entire cosmos.[11]

So our ancestors, in seeking to find life on their own terms, lost the author of all of life and tragically reversed the point of their own creation. That life was not first about some sort of utopian-esque pursuit or some human-made vision of becoming but eternal life spent being with God.

This tragic reversal had dramatic consequences for humanity as they were driven out of God's very presence. We are told, "Therefore the Lord God sent him out from the garden of Eden to work the ground from which he was taken. He drove out the man...." Notice the intensifying of language as we are first told they are "sent" but then a sentence later we see God "drove" them out of His presence. This story is intensifying and spiraling out of control. Whatever the people had become was leading to this situation snowballing out of control as the Father now has to personally send His creation out of His very presence.

A movement that is driven by humans as they travel further and further away from the goal of their creation. As they are driven out, we see "at the east of the garden of Eden he placed the cherubim and a flaming sword." God would place guardians to protect the east side of the garden so humans could no longer make the western journey towards Eden (which totally explains why the West Coast is the best coast. Sorry not sorry, East Coast readers). Humanity continued to spiral away from God at this point which is marked in the biblical narrative by a journey east.

The eastward journey would be one repeated throughout the biblical story. After subsequent biblical stories (following Genesis 3) about the first murder, rising human depravity leading to a worldwide flood that restarted the human project, and humanity gathering together to build a tower that would have its "top in the heavens" in an attempt to "make a name for ourselves", we see each part of the story marked as a "people moved eastward."[12] East becomes the marker to tell the reader that humanity continues to move into deeper levels of autonomy and self apart from the end to which they were created. *Humans descend further into becoming human doings, not human beings.*

Ultimately, the most dramatic consequence of our story is found in the last verse of Genesis 3. God places "the cherubim and a flaming sword that turned every way to guard the way to the tree of life." God would place these angelic critters to guard the way to where life was found and ultimately access to the Giver of all of life. So due to the decisions of our ancestors, our people had lost their way, becoming exiles and wanderers in a foreign land away from Eden.

Unable to find consolation.
Forever destined to scroll.
Having lost life.

But did they *really* lose life? Because they still seem fairly alive despite the circumstances. They even got a parka out of it. Not so bad until we go back to earlier in our story. In the narrative, Adam and Eve were told directly from God that if they ate from the tree of knowledge of good and evil that "for in the day you eat of it you shall surely die."[13] This seems *very* clear.

Death.
Destruction.
Cable television.

The serpent's crafty lie to our ancestors was clearly that "you will not surely die."[14] Was the serpent right? Adam and Eve did not die immediately and actually lived quite long lives (930 years to be exact. I have no idea what to do with that. Maybe in my next book?). What if the serpent was right and wrong at the same time (sort of like no king but there really was a king the whole time). The crafty serpent was right in the sense that Adam and Eve did not immediately experience physical death when they ate from the tree of the knowledge of good and evil. Yet he was gravely wrong at the same time as Adam and Eve experienced a death deeper and darker than physical death could ever be. They experienced the death of the ability to just be, and they lost the ability to just go walking with their Father.

Therefore, they didn't experience literal death but experienced the even worse death of a separation and alienation away from God Himself. See, *death isn't scary but death away from God is* as the creation was destined to live life perpetually away from their Creator. They had *become* like their Creator but could no longer *be* with Him. A people who had gained the whole world but lost their souls (or, more so, the Creator of their souls).[15]

In this tragic tale, we find the telos of our lives. Originally, humans were created in the image of God and created "like God" in the beginning. Yet in an ironic turn they continued the quest to become further like God choosing to eat from the tree of the knowledge of good and evil. Focusing solely on self, lowering their eyes and trying to get on the level of God. To acquire wisdom independent of Him birthed in the lies of the crafty serpent. The great irony in this pursuit was that they became like God, but they missed the ultimate point of their creation....(drum roll please)....*to be with God.*

This is the greatest tragedy of the fall as **the fundamental goal of our lives is to "be" with God.**

No goal or rival telos is more central to our shared humanity than this. *The pursuit of deep meaning and purpose is not first found in becoming like God but in being with God as His presence is the proper place to become like Him and live for Him.*[16]

No form of becoming at its core has value within itself. As we have seen from Dallas Willard in *The Spirit of the Disciplines*: "Yet when we look closely and continually at Jesus, we do not lose sight of this one fundamental, crucial point—the activities constituting the disciplines *have no value in themselves.* The aim and substance of spiritual life is not fasting, prayer, hymn singing, frugal living, and so forth. *Rather, it is the effective and full enjoyment of active love of God and humankind in all the daily rounds of normal existence where we are placed.*"[17]

The disciplines (he means spiritual disciplines or spiritual practices) *have no value in themselves.* Nothing. Nada. Now, he isn't saying that these good practices or habits don't matter or that we should throw out all discipline (don't worry, Jocko), but that they mean nothing without being placed in proper alignment with the presence of God. We get this when we start thinking about various disciplines and practices.

We could spend weeks in prayer like ascetics in church history yet our words can so easily turn into mere ritual or empty religiosity without relationship with God as the proper context.

We could preach breathtaking sermons about the glory, greatness, and grandeur of God, yet have cold and unreceptive hearts without regular calibration to the One we preach about in the first place.

We could sell all we have, give the money to save the sea turtles and move into a tiny home, yet without the Presence, we would sit in our tiny home absolutely distracted.

Point being, all of these practices have value only to the end which they were created for. They are all a means to an end. Us moderns have merely recycled through the classic human problem since the very beginning; *constructing a way of life where we become without being.*

Leading to the full gambit of criticisms from our pals like....
....Pascal....
....Judges....
....and Nietzsche.

Yet, what if we did something different from our ancestors? Could we discover the real invitation at hand in this narrative? To put being before becoming. To awake a generation from a distracted slumber. To unearth the very end which we were created for as the *telos* of our lives. To rediscover the sacred art of *being* with God.

§

There it is. Now you know. The cat's out of the bag and we can all be done with this journey. **The fundamental goal of our lives is to be with God.** I wish I had some new, novel concept for you but honestly I don't (unfortunately, this is also why I'm not going to get a cool Netflix documentary like Brene Brown). This isn't new and really has been the word on the street since, well, the *beginning* of time itself (yeah, a really long time). I don't think you're all that disappointed; we know that many times the deepest truths are the simple ones that were right in front of us all along.

This central truth of being with God has been the fundamental one that helped me rediscover my first love. All of the spiritual disciplines and practices are helpful, but they only helped me when I was able to put them in their proper place, which is the Presence. This is vital because even doing tons of good and godly things can burn us out when they're not placed in alignment with being with God. An all to common lifestyle that is built on becoming like God and doing things for Him while forgetting the radical invitation of being with Him as our primary aim.

At this point, we still have a big problem. We get the person of the Father in our story and we get that the point of our lives is to be with God. Yet we are left right now with humans dramatically missing the point and being driven out of God's very presence. I mean, this can't be the end of the story.

With this in mind, let's turn to the redemptive *plan* of God to bring the full and effective restoration of the purpose of the *presence* which is the goal and trajectory of the entire biblical story.

Chapter 5

Presence

A while back my son Ephraim and I went walking. This was a new rhythm for us as he had just learned to walk on his own (praise Jesus because he was getting way too heavy to carry). Our walk together led us to our local "everything is organic, paper bags are the spawn of Satan, everything is way overpriced but they know we will still buy it because we're total urban snobs" grocery store (got to love Seattle life).

As we were walking into the store, the doors automatically flung open and Ephraim instantly darted the other way. He wanted no part of that voodoo Harry Potter juju magic that caused the automatic doors to open. It honestly took me a minute to figure out what had happened, and it makes a lot of sense if you think about it. Never had he walked through automatic doors on his own, so he had no framework for how they actually worked (I tried to explain mechanical engineering to him, but that was a step or two above his usual books about random zoo animals).

So of course I walked over to him and tried to

demonstrate how the doors worked. As he stood 10 feet away, crying, I showed him how the doors effortlessly opened on their own when one approached them. I could see the gears shifting in his mind as he was trying to understand this great mystery. In response to my magical demonstration, Ephraim slowly walked up to the doors like he was trying to catch them off guard, crouching tiger style. Once he got a few feet away, the doors opened like usual. He ran backwards again, but he was a little closer and a little bolder this time.

Once again, I went back to him and showed him that there was nothing to fear. I could see his ever growing boldness and the trust in his eyes. So in response, Ephraim sprinted up to the doors as fast as possible in an attempt to once again catch them off guard. As he did this, they opened automatically and he stopped a foot away, just staring at them. I could tell he was starting to get how this whole thing worked (and all the typical Seattleites who walked by with no kids were reminded why they just have dogs).

Finally, Ephraim took his original mark about 10 feet away and got into a pseudo sprinter stance. You could see the sheer determination and focus on his brow as he took off towards the automatic doors (seriously, this might as well have been a Gatorade commercial). As he kept getting closer and closer, it became readily apparent that he had zero intention of stopping. I began interceding to the Father that this wouldn't be the only time in my life that automatic doors stopped working (if not, we could at least get on *America's Funniest Home Videos* and my son would only need a few years of counseling to deal with the trauma).

As Ephraim got close, the doors opened wide and he pressed through the doorway like a sprinter giving all he had at the finish line. As he crossed the threshold of the doorway, he quickly turned around and looked at me with the biggest smile, proclaiming, "I did it!" All I could do was smile and rejoice with my son because he had pressed in and pressed through (I cried a little, too….well, actually a lot….because I am a total crier. This was the first time he walked through automatic doors on his own. I definitely still need to make a scrapbook about this moment).

This moment, though, was much deeper than him

merely passing through a set of doors. What really resonated was that *my son had passed through the threshold of his fears to embrace a posture of faith.* A faith that trusted his father's word above all else and believed the doors would open when he finally decided to go through. A decision to accept the clarion call to press in and press through even when he didn't know what the end result would be. A call that goes out to each one of us no matter where we find ourselves.

An invitation to each of us today to press in to the Father's very presence. An invitation, not only in our faith but also our fear, to go walking once again. An invitation that beckons us to trust the Father's character and to orient all of our lives *around the practice of the presence of God.* But will we go walking with our Father?

This is a fundamental posture that we need to rediscover from the people of the past. Brother Lawerence, a 17th century French monk, postured his life in this manner. For decades, he would cultivate the art of being in the monastery kitchen where he worked (he and I have a lot in common in terms of our household responsibilities). He would give his days to the tedious chores of cooking and cleaning at the constant bidding of his superiors. In this place, he developed his own rule of spirituality and work. Because of the posture of his life, the higher ups at the monastery would send people to come and interview him to understand how he had found such a deep peace (a peace that I have yet to find while doing dishes). This led Brother Lawerence to grant only four interviews in his lifetime, and they were translated into a short book titled *The Practice of the Presence of God*.

This book is centrally about a call to the Presence in the nooks and crannies of the normalcy of life. Brother Lawerence would say this about his fundamental posture: "The time of business does not with me differ from the time of prayer; and in the noise and clatter of my kitchen, while several persons are at the same time calling for different things, I possess God in as great tranquility as if I were upon my knees before the Blessed Sacrament."[1] Through the midst of his normal duties he had discovered the art of being. He learned that the ability to just be in the Presence was not somewhere out there in the ethereal realm or merely relegated to being up in heaven but in the here and now; amidst the busyness, he could have a sacred encounter. Heaven could meet earth in all of its glory in the ordinariness of life.

Amidst the chaos.
Amidst the scrolling.
Amidst the distractions.

A little piece of Heaven could come down and humanity could once again experience the fullness of the glory of God if humans would just press into the Presence.

The Presence that has been the invitation all along. *The Presence* that is the central telos of our lives. *The Presence* that is the focal point to God's unfolding plan for the cosmos. *The Presence* that brings us back to a garden called Eden.

§

Genesis 3:8 // And they heard the sound of the Lord God walking in the garden in the cool of the day....

In the beginning, God went *walking*. A reality we

have already seen as God came "walking in the garden in the cool of the day." God arrives on the scene yet humanity continues their eastward journey away from Him. Though the creation chose distance from the Creator, we see God continue to come walking at various points in the biblical story. After Genesis 3, the next time we see God come walking on the scene is found in a funky structure called the tabernacle found in the book of Leviticus (yup.... we're *finally* here. Pour the guji, please).

At the end of Leviticus, we see God redeclaring His divine goal to be among humans. God boldly declares, "I will make my dwelling among you."[2] God is going to dwell, and the Hebrew word for "dwelling" actually means tabernacle - a structure that enabled God's presence to be with his people as it was meant to be a microcosm and mirror of Eden itself. In the tabernacle, God's presence would dwell in the western side of the tabernacle, guarded by cherubim and the flaming sword. Its rooms were designed with a tree-like lampstand at the center and with trees all around that were crafted like the tree of life.[3]

The tabernacle's entire structure was created as

a mini-Eden where Heaven would meet Earth, inviting humans to make the pilgrimage back to the very presence of God. In this place and space, God would once again go walking. At the end of Leviticus, God declared, "I will walk among you."[4] The last time in the entire story of the scriptures that this word was used was when God went walking in the Garden with Adam and Eve in Genesis 3:8. Can anybody say *remix*?

Volume 2:
God Walking.

Featuring weird sacrifices, men with flowing beards dressed up in really elaborate robes and that whole goat thing (this must be some sort of reality TV show). I mean the Father is *still* desiring to commune with His kids. But it's a little different now and seems a bit distant.

I guess this is what we get when an absolutely holy and perfect Father is trying to find a way to dwell with His imperfect and sinful kids. But hey - it's something. The heart of the matter is that the tabernacle was a sacred space enabling God to go walking among His people once again. So, though

Leviticus seems really strange to us moderns, its ultimate goal was not about God adding obscure and strange rituals to human life but creating a way for His people to return to Eden. God's people would fully be with their God as they were back in the beginning (well, sort of like the beginning).

The intention of this return to Eden in the tabernacle would be marked once again by the closeness of God and humans. After first speaking of walking, God says, "I will walk among you and will be your God, and you shall be my people."[5] This is a statement that will be picked up again and again throughout the entire Bible as the chorus about the intricate relationship that the Creator desires with His creation. A declaration of how God will bring His purposes and plan to fruition in the world as it was supposed to be all along. No matter the ups and downs, God's presence would be with His people through thick and thin.

Yet we know in the biblical story that humans continue to do the same things that they did in the very beginning. God's people settle into rhythms of deep idolatry and injustice, creating further and further depths of separation. So much so that it led to judgment and ultimately exile out of the Promised Land into the hands of foreign nations and oppressors. One ends the Old Testament story wondering, when will God go walking with His humans once again? When will the intimacy of God and humans be restored? Or could this be the end of the story?

The Lord God eternally destined to go walking by Himself. Forever destined to eat pints of Ben & Jerry's and watch cable television. How would God ever cross this vast divide as His humans prove again and again their total inability to go walking with Him?

We find an unlikely answer in the dramatic claim of the Gospel writers. The author known as John writes in the introduction of his Gospel, "And the Word became flesh and dwelt among us."[6] John opens his Gospel with a radical statement about a person named "the Word." To us, this seems like a strange introduction, yet it was a mark of sheer brilliance to John's contemporaries. "The Word" means *logos* in Greek and served as a vital concept in John's day. In the 1st century, the Greeks believed that the universe had a rational and moral order to it and they called this order of nature the logos. The Greeks would spend their lives philosophizing and contemplating the existential goal of humanity which for them was the very meaning of life.

So, John skillfully and purposefully takes this cultural concept and applies it in a revolutionary way. John doesn't fundamentally describe the logos as an abstract principle or philosophy, but as a person who actually walked on earth. *Making the profound point that the meaning of life was not found in some abstract philosophy or principle, but in a person.*

This idea was one of the very turning points in all of human thought as the world had never seen this concept before. Pastor Tim Keller writes, "If Christianity was true, a well-lived life was not found primarily in philosophical contemplation and intellectual pursuits, which would leave out most of the people in the world. Rather, it was found in a person to be encountered in a relationship that could be available to anyone, anywhere, from any background."[7] Fundamentally, John picked up on a revolutionary invitation in his cultural moment to *all* people - that the meaning of life was found in an actual person who actually walked on earth....a person named Jesus who invites all people to go walking.

But this invitation was not necessarily brand new as Jesus was not just the meaning of life but the fulfillment of God's very promises to His people since the very beginning. John makes this clear as he writes, "....the Word became flesh and dwelt among us."[8] This word "dwelt" is a word we have read before in Leviticus, simply meaning to tabernacle and more literally "He pitched His tabernacle among us." God tabernacled among humanity and His tabernacling presence was now found in a person who was walking on Earth. Much like in the Old Testament story of how God came walking in the Garden and again in the tabernacle, we see God walking among humans but in a very literal way since He actually had two legs.

A moment that seemed....
....so unlikely.
....so unexpected.
....so unanticipated.

So needed as Jesus fulfilled where we failed. Jesus was the one who displayed "his glory, glory as of the only Son from the Father, full of grace and truth."[9] "Glory" is a significant marker for us in the biblical story as glory is a central word that connects us back to when God's very presence would come down in the tabernacle (and subsequent temple). John is dramatically saying, "You remember when our ancestors would see the Presence come down back in the day? Yeah, it's here....or more so, *He's* here."

Theologian G.K. Beale aptly summarizes John's legendary point as "the special revelatory presence of God, formerly contained in the holy of holies of the tabernacle and temple, has now burst forth into the world in the form of the incarnate God, Jesus Christ."[10] Through Jesus, we are seeing the fulfillment of God's promise to go walking with humans *as Jesus became a human to enable humanity to go walking with God.*

Volume 3:
God Walking.

Minus the obscure laws, men with beards, and goats being cast into the wilderness. Just a person. A person who achieved our telos in our place and on our behalf to enable us to once again go walking with our Father. A holy invitation to rediscover how to just be if we will fix our eyes on the founder and perfecter of our faith....Jesus.[11]

Yet if we are being honest with ourselves, even on our best days when we follow Jesus we can still struggle to be at times (as seen in me losing my first love).

Struggling with....
....scrolling.
....distraction.
....Netflix binges.

I don't mean to say that just because we trust Jesus that we will have it all together or perfectly go walking with God everyday into eternity (especially not on those days when we're awoken at 3:59 AM). Because we can all think of those times when someone told us we just needed to "trust" God a bit more and were like, "what in the world am I supposed to do?"

To make sense of the days we live in, it is imperative to acknowledge that we live between what theologians call the *now and not yet*. As

John pointed out to us 2,000 years ago, the death and resurrection of Jesus fundamentally changed everything for humans as Jesus ushered in heaven on earth. Because of Jesus' death and resurrection, we are invited into a direct relationship with God through the person of Jesus. But we also eagerly wait in anticipation for a day when Jesus will come again to renew and restore all things. There is still a fulfillment to come that will bring the consummation and full summation of God's plan on earth.

A plan that is fulfilled on the last pages of the story of scripture. On the last page of the Bible we are brought to *the* final vision of the renewal of all things. John writes in Revelation 21, "Then I saw a new heaven and a new earth."[12] John is given an apocalyptic, prophetic vision about the days to come. A vision that is in no way about humans being beamed up out of this world or about how the world is going to hell in a handbasket but of heaven coming down to earth in one glorious moment when heaven and earth would meet like in Eden.[13]

In John's final climactic vision, we see the full fulfillment of God's promises to humanity. John tells us that the purpose of this universal, cosmic renewal is that "the dwelling place of God is with humans."[14] Again, God's dwelling is with humans. This is the same word we have seen throughout our story as the word "dwelling" means tabernacle. So in this picture, the entire restorative work of God in the cosmos is a cosmic version of the tabernacle of God representing *a return to Eden*. At the very center of this restorative work are many ties with the garden of Eden, but one of the central pictures is the tree of life at the very center bringing healing to all of the nations.[15] Humanity has come full circle and God has brought His renewal to the world so that God and humans can go walking once again.

Volume 4:
God Walking.

Hand-in-hand into eternity. An eternal chorus on repeat (while "Everything is Awesome" is banished into the lake of fire for eternal torment). A day where we will be fully immersed in God's very presence. A day that is *the* trajectory of the entire cosmos. A day where we will fully be with God. This joyful, triumphant day will be the consummation of the closeness that God has always desired with His people. John writes, "....and they will be His people, and God Himself will be with them as their God."[16] A line we have heard before all the way back in Leviticus that echoes to us that God will fulfill His promises, even to the bitter end. That God's people would finally and fully be immersed in the very presence of God.

At this point it becomes clear that the trajectory of the entire story of God (and of the cosmos) is that humans would be with God. It is evident that "the telos for Christians is Christ: Jesus Christ is the very embodiment of what we're made for, of the end to which we are called."[17] Jesus is the telos of our lives and his invitation is to orient our lives around the practice of the Presence in the here and now. To see heaven come down to earth. To see God's glory break into the mundane. To fulfill our full destiny among the distractions.

That we would fully and effectively be able to enjoy God forever.[18] That we would finally be able to go *walking* with our Father. That nothing would keep us from the *Presence*.

§

This vision has been *the* vision that has helped me pilgrimage back to my first love and form the vision that has kept my soul from wandering ever since. A *plan* that God set out since the beginning of time to bring humanity back into His presence. A plan that does mean automatic perfection or that we will have it all figured out but that our souls have been so gripped by a vision that is so immense, so compelling, so beautiful that we will never find an end to the adventure that is being with God.

A vision that we so desperately need now. Antoine de Saint-Exupéry, the writer of *The Little Prince*, once profoundly declared, "If you want to build a ship don't drum up people to collect wood and don't assign them tasks and work, but rather teach them to long for the endless immensity of the sea."[19] *Teach them to long*. To not focus on all of the tasks or busy work, but to first create a vision that causes one's soul to long for more.

A vision that stirs up....
....a deep desire.
....a deep longing.
....a deep yearning.

To be with God. To spend all of our remaining days fully immersed in and enamored by the very presence of God. To press forward with all we have in the valleys of despair and distraction towards the mountain top of God's restorative and renewing work when all will stand before this throne, forever destined to just be with Him.

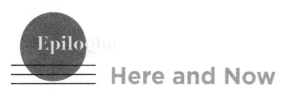

Here and Now

What to make of the *here and now?*

To be honest, my natural instinct is to write a manifesto to you of how I'm really killin' the game at this whole being thing. To talk about how I can sit in a room with no windows, no sounds and no iPhone for weeks on end while I talk face-to-face with the manifest glory of the Lord God (and how God has given me a new set of laws to govern all of humanity through me as His very mediator to the world. Okay, so the last part has made things a little weird....and now potentially on the road to getting my own Netflix documentary).

But seriously, the here and now. Last weekend, Ephraim and I went to our local book store on the Sabbath. Third Place Books, to be exact (the place I go where I'm not drinking the guji). Now, I know what you're thinking....I take my three year old to book stores. I actually began the practice when he was about 6 months old and it's been hit or miss ever since. I have always struggled with the whole matching experience to the developmental stage of my child (sorry, Dr. Spock). I'm more so the "toss your kid in the deep end" kind of dad (like my father). Give'em something from Nietzsche or Pascal and see what happens. There are a lot of ways I can mess my kids up, but this seems on the *safer* end of childhood trauma (well, Nietzsche would definitely scar my children for life).

Anyways, so Ephraim and I rolled up to our local book store on the *Sabbath*.[1] A sacred practice that generations of the people of God have practiced for a few millennia. Every Friday night, we make a big dinner as a fam (well, more so my wife, but I do the dishes afterwards....we really aren't trying to feed into gender stereotypes). We all sit at the table with our delicious food, and as we sit there on the precipice of eating, we stop. Like totally just stop with forks in hand, to take a moment of silence as we light our Sabbath candle to invite God into the next 24 hours.

It's not really about just being with God for just 24 hours, but that we let one day a week set a trajectory for how our lives should always be in every moment of everyday. The Sabbath becomes the beginning of our week and sets our eyes on what really is essential in this whole thing we call life.

During these 24 hours, we have made a habit of learning to embrace *simplicity*. A posture of paring down our regular lifestyle and decluttering our lives. The clearest of this is seen through how we basically become Amish for a whole 24 hours when it comes to all things technology. I intentionally take up the spiritual practice of forgetting my iPhone wherever I go (to the dismay of my wife when she actually needs something from me).

Now this doesn't mean distractions don't ever come up or that we never pull out our iPhones. It means that we are intentionally committing to a different lifestyle that's centered on slowing ourselves down to capture a new way of being in our technologically driven world. So on this sleepy Saturday, I left my phone at home and Ephraim + I went to the bookstore.

While at the bookstore I always actively work at learning the sacred practice of *slowing*. Something about books helps me really live this practice. I love the feel of books, I love turning through their pages and I even love the smell of a good worn book (yes, you're not the only one). So, I spend way too long every Sabbath slowing down to the pace of the written word. Maybe that's why books are so good for slowing?

No pop-ups or click bait.
No social media trying to suck out my soul.
No franticness or chaos of the current news cycle.

But a measured and slow encounter as I meander through the rows of books. Now-a-days (at times) I even allow myself to wander into the fiction section. A strange and dangerous place that very few like me venture.

A place of whimsey.
A place of curiosity.
A place of stories.

Ugh.

Who's got time for all these stories when you've got things to do? I've got a world to change. We need more books that can actually help move the ball forward for all of humanity.

Allowing myself to wander through these sacred rows has only arisen from this journey of being as bookstores used to be a place of great anxiety. I used to literally be in a row at the bookstore and get an idea out of nowhere about some sort of book I would write one day to make me rich and famous. I would instantly pull out my Moleskine journal dedicated to all my brilliant ideas. 30 seconds into my brainstorm session, I would have secured a publisher and have the launch date determined in my mind. A minute later I would be able to visualize that orange tab next to my book on Amazon that reads "Best Seller." 2 minutes later I would be an international best seller in 30 languages debating if I should do a podcast or not (the answer is always yes, of course).

I wrote an international best seller, so why not? I probably should get someone else to do it with me. Maybe Kanye? I am an international best-selling Christian author and he's now a Christian artist. It's a match made in heaven (if it's not clear already, this whole deep insecurity and inadequacy about who I am does flare up from time-to-time, especially during the Sabbath).

Yet in the midst of my insecurity, I stop my soul and recalibrate by the practice of *silence*. A silence I usually find by walking to one of my favorite coffee shops near the bookstore. I grab a good cup of guji and a blueberry scone for Ephraim (+ one for Abram as well. Yeah, Hilary and I have done the whole "be fruitful and multiply" thing. It's starting to get *really* expensive to go out).

As I sit down, I close my eyes, control the pace of my breathing and invite the Spirit of God afresh to breathe worth and value into the deep places of insecurity and inadequacy that want more when I attempt to stop achieving and embrace being. In the silence, I remind myself of the way of Jesus that has not captured the world's imagination from generation-to-generation by force, but through "the unforced rhythms of grace."[2]

These regular practices are at the core of how I pattern my life to the art of being. They are not the only practices that I have tried, but they are starting places for learning to reorient one's life. Honestly, I wish I could give you some sort of easy self-helpy next steps to completely change your life overnight. Some sort of *12 Steps to Just Be RIGHT NOW* (seriously, that would have been the book I wrote back in the day because that would be really efficient for both of us). Yet I know it would not be helpful, and it would further feed into the culture of how-to that is so pervasive in our cultural moment.

As I have already made clear, we don't need another how-to. We need a new vision for how to fundamentally understand the entire goal of our lives as our deepest desires are uncovered in the act of being. A fundamental recalibration to a new way of life and love found in the way of Jesus.

§

At this point, there is nothing else to ask other than *will you join me?* Before each of us awaits the greatest invitation in all of the world. **To be with God.**

No matter if this feels like our first or ten thousandth attempt at being, we can know with complete confidence and certainty that we have a God who wants to go walking with us.

Or more so, *you.* Yes, you. Where you are in the here

and now. Not some future picture of you, but you as you stand in your imperfections.

You who struggles with self.
You who scrolls way too much.
You who can't seem to focus your eyes.

That you is *the* one the Creator of the cosmos desires to be with. A fact that brings solace for our souls.

To be able to rediscover our *first love*.
To be able to recalibrate *2 degrees* at a time.
To be able to stop *scrolling* and focus on our true *Father*.
To be able to know the very *telos* we were created for in the *Presence*.
To be able to learn the art of being in the *here and now*.

Conclusion

2020

2020.

What else do I have to say? A year that conjures up images of endless Zoom calls, the designer mask market springing up out of nowhere and the whole world trying to survive through a global pandemic (and that whole no pants thing we started this book with). I am not sure if we will ever have a year like 2020 again, but if we did, this is your invitation to learn how to 2020-proof your life for the future. Sort of like being a doomsday prepper who buys all of the toilet paper at Costco (and most likely has endless amounts of Spam in an underground bunker….very likely).

Okay, so maybe not that extreme but you get the idea. That we can actually prepare our hearts and minds ahead of time through the intentional practice of learning to be. We don't have to wait for our lives to fall apart or for another global pandemic to hit to figure this all out but we can let 2020 be the impetus to make a change now.

So to 2020-proof your life, I wanted to recommend a few good reads on a few central spiritual practices for your further exploration (I know, I'm a total nerd….who recommends more books after making you read an entire book? Worst teacher move ever).

You don't have to read all of them (I know you won't) but pick up one of these on a practice that stands out to you and let that be the place you begin to 2020-proof your life, embracing the radical posture of being.

SABBATH

The Sabbath by Abraham Joshua Heschel - A short classic written by a Jewish theologian who was one of the top Hebrew minds of the 20th century. It is a literary masterpiece that will rewrite your categories for how you understand time itself.

Subversive Sabbath by A.J. Swoboda - A book full of scriptural connections to the Sabbath that I have seen very few connect. Stuff like how the practice of the Sabbath relates to the economy, the marginalized, creation care, etc.

SIMPLICITY

Digital Minimalism by Cal Newport - Technology so easily slips into the practice of simplicity. Newport's work is masterful and he has a good balance of general philosophical approach and tangible practices.

The Ruthless Elimination of Hurry by John Mark Comer - Comer's chapter on simplicity is one of the best works I have read on the practice and is worth the price of admission. John Mark also has a really tangible workbook on how to unhurry your life that is so helpful (and totally free): https://johnmarkcomer.com/blog/unhurry.

Essentialism by Greg McKeown - I am not sure if I have found a book that has more accurately helped me depict my general life approach. McKeown's writing will primarily help you discover simplicity in your overall life calling as well as help you align your daily habits with the vision of being.

SLOWING

Present Over Perfect by Shauna Niequist - The title sort of says it all (yea, let the conviction settle in as you read it). Niquist's writing is a beautiful, whimsical journey into slowing down our souls to a simpler, more soulful way of life.

The Emotionally Healthy Leader (or Emotionally Healthy Spirituality) by Peter Scazzero - There is an entire set of books around the emotionally healthy life from Scazzero but either one of these two is a great place to start. The entire book basically messed me up (as I cried page-by-page) but his chapter on *Slow Down for Loving Union* is where I would hone in on for this practice.

The Gift of Being Yourself by David Benner - This may seem like a strange add to the list as it is not directly about the practice of slowing yet I am not sure if anything but the process of self-discovery could be more core to actually slowing down. Benner's book is a short invitation to the lifelong process of acceptance and love.

Invitation to Solitude and Silence by Ruth Haley Barton - A masterful starting place for receiving the invitation to silence and solitude. Honestly, I can't think of a better and more readable place to begin than in Barton's work. She has a whole plethora of books that relate to this subject as well.

Celebration of Discipline by Richard Foster - This book is more general than just the practice of silence & solitude, but is a classic in reading about spiritual formation. Foster has chapters on meditation, prayer and solitude that would all be beneficial for this practice.

I know I just gave you 10 books (cheers) but don't freak out as we literally just spent an entire book talking about how the goal of our lives is to be. But all I can say is, start *somewhere*.

Somewhere gets the ball rolling. Somewhere is always a great place to begin. Somewhere leads us out of being nowhere to the process of discovering greener pastures. Somewhere puts the focus on putting one foot in front of the other and letting the journey unfold (remember this is basically how we all survived 2020).

Day-by-Day.
Week-by-Week.
Month-by-Month.
Year-by-Year.

Of learning to *2020*-proof our lives.

Thanks

Thank you, Hil. You really are my first love and continuously bring me back to our true first love. Also you did all of the design for this entire book (yea....I married up).

Abe + E, I love you. If anything, this is a bunch of words meant to convey my love + God's love for you. You have taught me more than anyone else about how to just be (+ how to act like a really scary T-Rex).

Mom + Dad (in heaven), thank you for showing me what a real father and mother look like (I was only slightly messed up which is a whole heck of a lot better than most).

I have many influences + voices in my writing, but special thanks go to Dr. Gerry Breshears as much of the narrative of Genesis came alive as I sat in your classes.

Kardia fam, you know who you are. Yes, God only gave us a season to walk together but what a ride we had (and a special thanks for our *Bachelor* watch nights as it clearly inspired much of my work).

MC4 thank you for your continued encouragement throughout this process and providing a place for my soul to find deep rest, healing, and renewal (seriously your awesome!).

Blake, Grant and Dr. J - thank you for your encouragement and much needed feedback throughout this process. Extra special thanks to Emily for diving all-in on line-by-line editing and helping shape this work to what it is now.

Lastly, thank you Jesus (imagine me pointing to heaven Tim Tebow style). Seriously, I have been compelled to write because of your majesty, grandeur and ever-pursuing love. You spoke the word to write my story and all I can do is put it before you as my submission to your gracious voice.

Discussion

Below are discussion questions for each chapter to help you + a group of friend's further consider and have conversation around the ideas in each chapter as well as to begin to put them into practice. Enjoy!

Chapter 1: 2 Degrees

1. The story of the steamship *Monroe* ramming the merchant vessel *Nantucket* was not merely about the tragic loss of life but an example of the consequences of being a little off over a long period of time. What are examples that come to mind when you think of the consequences of being 2 degrees off?

2. In this chapter, Trevor writes, "The seeds of our own destruction are ever present in the habits of our daily lives." How does this understanding of spiritual compromise change how we view our spiritual growth? The growth of those we invest into?

3. Pastor Eugene Peterson describes the Christian life as "a long obedience in the same direction." What is the connection between the presence of God and daily spiritual practices or disciplines (obedience)?

4. The opening chapters of Genesis introduce us to a picture of God as both transcendent and immanent. In what ways does this picture of God challenge or affirm how you currently understand God? Which aspect of God (as transcendent or immanent) do you find more challenging to grasp onto? Why?

5. Throughout the opening verses of Genesis 3, the subtleness of the serpent's words and Eve's ever shifting response becomes readily apparent. What portion of the serpent's words or Eve's response struck you? Why?

6. Practice // Fixed-Hour Prayer - Designate three times a day (morning, midday, evening) when you will stop to be with God for the next week. Don't think of these times as long durations of time but 10 minute increments where you will stop to integrate being into the normal rhythms and routines of your day.

Chapter 2: Scrolling

1. How do you normally wake up in the morning? Ready to take on the world or hating life until a good cup of coffee? Something in-between?

2. We live in an age saturated in technology and social media. How do you see the effects of scrolling (and social media) play out in your own experience? Those close to you? If not technology, what distracts you from being actively aware of God's presence?

3. Shauna Niequist in her Facebook post invited us to the reality that "you can just be human." How does her post make you feel? How can social media perpetuate a sense of striving and restlessness?

4. Living in a secular age broadly means being able to construct lives that focus purely on the immanent versus the transcendent. Do you think the critiques of our culture from Frederick Nietzsche, Charles Taylor and the author are fair? In what ways is our cultural moment similar and different then past generations?

5. The book of Judges connects the idea of having "no king" with humans "doing what is right in their own eyes." How do you see these ideas correlating? Give examples of how you see these ideas playing themselves out in culture today?

6. Trevor makes the case that "the deepest

temptation here is actually not to some sort of vice, but to virtue." Do you agree or disagree? What are examples of good intentions gone wrong?

7. Practice // Silence and Solitude - Carve out an extended time each day for the next week where you leave your smartphone in another room and spend 20 minutes in silence by yourself. As you begin each session simply pray, "Holy Spirit, I invite you into this place and space to speak in the silence."

Chapter 3: Father

1. Trevor points out that we can understand "father" in a biological sense but never really grasp it in a relational sense. Do you agree or disagree with this distinction? What are ways that people commonly struggle with the relational sense of a father?

2. Why do you think Jesus insisted upon using the term "Father" to describe God? What does this tell us about God's heart and His desire to interact with us?

3. Which aspect of God's response to Adam and Eve stood out to you the most? Is His response what you expected? In what ways did it challenge

your own conception of God as Father?

4. Adam responds to God coming on the scene by saying, "I heard the sound of you in the garden, and I was afraid, because I was naked, and I hid myself (Genesis 3:10)." How do you resonate with Adam's response to God? Give examples of how you see his response playing out in your own past experiences with God.

5. Brene Brown teaches, "Shame is a focus on self, guilt is a focus on behavior. Shame is, 'I am bad.' Guilt is, 'I did something bad.'" Do you agree or disagree with her dichotomy? How does this understanding change how you view past mistakes?

6. Practice // Confession - Each day this week spend time examining your own conscience and journal the experience. Ask the Father (God) to reveal things you have done, things that have been done to you, and things that have been done in your presence that impact you or others. Let yourself lament, determine new courses of action and be reminded of the Father's forgiveness for all mistakes.

Chapter 4: Telos

1. What is the difference between an app and an operating system? How does this distinction relate to the "why" and the "how" of our spiritual growth?

2. Trevor contends that, "It's hip to focus on finding one life hack to instantly change our lives versus spending intentional time focusing on the entire operating system that governs all of our core decisions." Do you agree or disagree? If so, why do you think people live more so consumed with the how-to's of our spiritual growth versus the deeper why?

3. God had told our ancestors that if they ate from the tree of the knowledge of good and evil that "you will surely die (Genesis 2:17)." The serpent would tell Eve, "You will surely not die (Genesis 3:4)." Who was right? What sort of death did Adam and Eve receive?

4. How does mixing up the order of being with God and becoming like God alter how we view and relate to God? Give one example of how changing the order of being/becoming would change a spiritual practice (for example in prayer or scripture

reading).

5. Dallas Willard states that, "the activities constituting the disciplines have no value in themselves." Do you agree or disagree with his assertion? Why or why not?

6. Practice // Sabbath - Attempt a 24-hour Sabbath this coming week. Before the day, process ways that you (and those you spend this day with like kid's or a spouse) can "pray" and "play." Determine a list of 3 things to do that would bring life and 3 things not to do that would take away from meaningful rest.

Chapter 5: Presence

1. Brother Lawerence in his classic *The Practice of the Presence of God* writes, "The time of business does not with me differ from the time of prayer." What do you think of breaking down this divide between what is sacred and secular? Where are opportunities to invite the presence of God into your normal routines and rhythms?

2. The biblical story picks up again and again in Leviticus, the Gospel of John and Revelation the idea of God "walking" on the scene. Which portion

of scripture of God "walking" stood out the most to you? Why?

3. Antoine de Saint-Exupéry, author of *The Little Prince*, wrote, "If you want to build a ship don't drum up people to collect wood and don't assign them tasks and work, but rather teach them to long for the endless immensity of the sea." Why is having a compelling vision so important for how we live everyday?

4. What do you sense the Spirit inviting you to do in response to the central vision presented in this book? What is one tangible next step you can take?

5. Practice // Re-visioning - Spend time everyday this week contemplating + journaling, "What kind of relationship do I want to have with God?" What is the most daring dream that comes from this processing? What actions would flow from such a relationship with God?

Notes

Pants in a Pandemic

1. Blaise Pascal, *Pensees* (New York City: Penguin Classics, 1995), 8.

2. Pascal, *Pensees*, 120.

3. Ladies, I will try to make everything gender neutral for terms that are clearly intended for men and women.

4. Pascal, *Pensees*, 37.

First Love

1. Italicized added. Dallas Willard, *The Spirit of the Disciplines: Understanding How God Changes Lives* (New York: HarperOne, 1988), 138. Other works from Willard that I love are *Renovation of the Heart* (Colorado Springs: NavPress, 2012) and *The Divine Conspiracy* (New York: HarperCollins, 1998).

2. I do want to add one important caveat here. I am totally inviting *you*, but this does not mean that you are the ending point of discovering how to be. *Our formation and growth is not just about me but we.* Two of my favs on this are Joseph Hellerman's *When the Church was a Family* (Nashville: B&H Publishing Group, 2009) and Mark Scandrette's *Practicing the Way of Jesus* (Downers Grove: InterVarsity Press, 2011). Bridgetown Church (in Portland) also has some incredible resources at https://practicingtheway.org on spiritual practices for small groups to work through together. I would highly recommend this journey be a communal experience versus mainly an individualistic one.

2 Degrees

1. "Monroe Steered by Faulty Compass," *New York Times*, February 12, 1914. I totally got this story from James K.A. Smith's, *You Are What You Love: The Spiritual Power of Habit* (Grand Rapids: Brazos Press, 2016), 20. I was debating using it since, well; he already used it. But then I realized that if stories are really good then it's worth telling more than once. Also, he writes quite intellectually and my readers (you) are all more likely to be binging on *The Bachelor* then reading Augustine (right there with you, my friend).
2. Aleksandr Solzhenitsyn, *The Gulag Archipelago: 1918-1956, Volume 2* (New York: Harper Perennial Modern Classics, 2007), 615-617.
3. Now to be clear, this does not dismiss these issues as matters of no consequence. Pope Benedict XVI began his first volume on the life of Jesus, *Jesus of Nazareth: From the Baptism in the Jordan to the Transfiguration* (New York: Doubleday, 2007), by addressing this tension when writing, "What did Jesus actually bring, if not world peace, universal prosperity, and a better world? What has he brought (44)?" Clearly the vision of the Kingdom of Heaven in-breaking into earth through the life and death of Jesus has social ramifications. Too often we can create a false dichotomy between what seems to be spiritual versus earthly matters. This has been a common story replayed again-and-again beginning in the

20th century with the Fundamentalist-Modernist debate until now. 20th century theologian Carl F.H. Henry, in his classic *The Uneasy Conscience of Modern Fundamentalism* (Grand Rapids: Eerdmans Publishing Company, 1947) prophetically wrote, "Fundamentalism in revolting against the Social Gospel seemed also to revolt against the Christian social imperative (22)." I think this all too common and my hope is not to further widen this chasm. Though I do want to reorient us in the midst of our cultural moment to the simple reality of what Pope Benedict XVI wrote in summarizing the life of Jesus, "What has [Jesus] brought? The answer is very simple: God. He has brought God (44)." Jesus has brought us access to God and I want to help us rediscover this core reality as the foundational step of our formation.

4. Special thanks to the sheer brilliance of *Stumptown Coffee™*.

5. This is the title of one of Peterson's well known books, *A Long Obedience in the Same Direction* (Downers Grove: InterVarsity Press, 2000). It actually wasn't my favorite book in the Peterson canon but the title is an incredible encapsulation of the heart of the discipleship journey. If you're looking for a Peterson book I would begin with *The Pastor* (New York: HarperOne, 2011) as it is one of my all-time fav's.

6. Alasdair MacIntyre, *After Virtue* (Notre Dame: University of Notre Dame Press, 2007), 216. Further resources for understanding the scriptures as a unified story are Craig Bartholomew and Michael Goheen's *The Drama of Scripture* (Grand Rapids: Baker Academic, 2014) as well as basically everything and anything *The Bible Project* puts out.

7. Genesis 1:1. Unless I say otherwise, all verses in this book will be from the *English Standard Version* (ESV).

8. Genesis 1:1. It is beyond the scope of this book to get into the debate on how long it specifically took God to create the world. If you're looking for more on this subject I would highly recommend John Sailhamer's *Genesis Unbound: A Provocative New Look at the Creation Account* (Colorado Springs: Dawson Media, 2011).

9. Scholars get into all sorts of weeds here about matters of authorship and the level of continuity/discontinuity actually at work in the narrative. If you're looking for an in-depth understanding of the history of biblical scholarship over the last few hundred years (especially with authorship in-mind), check out the first half of T. Desmond Alexander's *From Paradise to the Promised Land* (Grand Rapids: Baker Academic, 2012). If you are looking for a less historical recommendation but a more textual one - Stephen Dempster's *Dominion and Dynasty: A Theology of the Hebrew Bible* (Downers Grove: InterVarsity Press, 2003) is a fantastic starting place.

10. God saw - Genesis 1:4, 1:10, 1:12, 1:18, 1:25, 1:31. God said - Genesis 1:3, 1:6, 1:9, 1:11, 1:14, 1:20, 1:24, 1:26, 1:28, 1:29. God made - Genesis 1:7, 1:16, 1:25, 1:31. God called - Genesis 1:5, 1:8, 1:10. God created - Genesis 1:1. God blessed - Genesis 1:22, 1:28.

11. The Lord God formed the man - Genesis 2:7. The Lord God caused a deep sleep to fall upon the man - Genesis 2:21. The Lord God planted a garden...and there he put the man - Genesis 2:8. The Lord God took the man and put him in the garden of Eden to work and keep it - Genesis 2:15.

12. I first noticed this idea in the work of Alexander, *From*

Paradise to the Promised Land, 119-122.

13. Gordon J. Wenham, *Word Biblical Commentary Genesis 1-15* (Waco: Word Books, 1987), 72.

14. Genesis 2:24

15. Genesis 2:9+16-17

16. Genesis 2:16

17. Genesis 2:17

Scrolling

1. I actually do not keep my iPhone on my night stand anymore. I realized how important environmental design is for our formation. James Clear in *Atomic Habits* (New York: Avery, 2018) writes, "Environment is the invisible hand that shapes human behavior (82)." Andy Crouch in his fantastic book, *The Tech-Wise Family* (Grand Rapids: Baker Books, 2017), develops this idea with technology specifically in mind in his principle, "We want to create more than we consume. So we fill the center of our home with things that reward skill and active engagement (71)." Both of these are hitting on a similar idea around designing your living space intentionally with your best life in mind.

2. Jocko Willink, (@jockowillink), March 15th, 2019, 8:30 PM.

3. The Bucket List Family, (@thebucketlistfamily), March 9th, 2019, 9 PM.

4. Colton Underwood, (@coltonunderwood), March 29th, 2019, 7:30 PM.

5. Shauna Niequist, (@sniequist), January 4th 2019, 7:04 AM.

6. Frederick Nietzsche, *The Gay Science* (New York: Vintage, 1974), 181-182. Charles Taylor in *A Secular Age* (Cambridge/ London: The Belknap Press of Harvard University Press, 2007) summarizes the meaning of "the death of God" in the modern consciousness writing, "one essential idea which this phrase captures is that conditions have arisen in the modern world in which it is no longer possible, honestly, rationally, without confusions, or fudging, or mental reservation, to believe in God. These conditions leave us nothing we can believe in beyond the human--human happiness, or potentialities, or heroism (560)."

7. Taylor, *A Secular Age*, 18. This is not where I would begin with understanding secularism and the cultural moment we live in. Here is my recommended list of resources in-order: 1) Heather Grizzle & Jon Tyson's *A Creative Minority* + *This Cultural Moment* podcast by John Mark Comer + Mark Sayers. 2) Mark Sayers *Disappearing Church* (Chicago: Moody Publishers, 2016) + *Reappearing Church* (Chicago: Moody Publishers, 2019). 3) James K.A. Smith's *How (Not) To Be Secular* (Grand Rapids: William B. Eerdmans Publishing Company, 2014). 4) The magnum opus on secularism by Taylor, *A Secular Age*.

8. This is basically what Taylor writes in *A Secular Age*, "A race of humans has arisen which has managed to experience its world entirely as immanent. In some respect, we may judge this achievement as a victory for darkness, but it is a remarkable achievement nonetheless (376)."

9. My point is *not* that the stewardship of the earth or justice for indigenous peoples doesn't matter but that these worthy pursuits are not enough to bring fulfillment within themselves apart from a connection to God. All too often in-response to a deep sense of inadequacy and unfulfillment, we continually search for matters of *immanence* to fulfill us in areas where we need *transcendence*. So we jump from issue to issue trying to find meaning. We get a "hit" of fulfillment from our most recent tweet against injustice yet it is not enough to produce lasting staying power as the deep sense of being "haunted" never goes away leading us to never actually commit to a regular pattern and posture of living justly. To develop a life patterned around matters of justice I would contend that a life centered on the transcendent (a life spent being with Jesus) actually gives us a long-lasting vision for active engagement in the immanent. 19th-20th century Dutch Prime Minister, Pastor, and Theologian Abraham Kuyper famously proclaimed, "There is not a square inch in the whole domain of our human existence over which Christ, who is sovereign over all, does not cry 'Mine!'" This understanding of God's presence should propel us to be more consistently engaged in matters of justice as Jesus is Lord over all spheres of social, political, and economic life. Therefore, a life spent intimately with Jesus *must* propel us to do what Jesus did.

10. Isaiah 9:6

11. This does not undermine that technology is a critically important arena for followers of Jesus to consider when we talk about our formation. Generally I would recommend anything that the *Center for Humane Technology* puts out. Especially their podcast as they propose that most tech firms only ask the questions of what and how but never why one should create a certain technology. From a faith perspective, I would begin with Tony Reinke's *12 Ways Your Phone is Changing You* (Wheaton: Crossway, 2017) or Crouch's *The Tech-Wise Family* (Crouch is where I would start for families).

12. Moral corruption - Judges 2:19. Child sacrifices - Judges 11. The pillaging of innocent villages - Judges 18. Rape and sexual abuse - Judges 19:25.

13. Judges 20

14. Judges 17:6, 18:1, 19:1, 21:25

15. 1 Samuel 8:7 - 1 Samuel is the book right after Judges in the scriptures.

16. The statement of there being "no king" during the time of Judges can be read as a straight forward observation that there was literally no earthly king over Israel during the time of Judges as the people were governed by local tribal chieftains. Christopher J.H. Wright in *Here Are Your Gods* (Downers Grove: InterVarsity Press, 2020) points out that reading the text this way would "imply that perhaps, if only they could get a really strong king ("like all the other nations"), then that would solve the problems of idolatry, social fracturing, and insecurity (102)." As he points out, this reading would seem to miss the point seen through God's commentary on this time in 1 Samuel and the disastrous results that would come with Israel actually being given a monarchy seen in the rest of the Old Testament story. In *Judges & Ruth* (Brazos Theological Commentary) (Grand Rapids: Brazos Press, 2018), Laura A. Smit writes, "The book of Judges is concerned not so much with the absence of a human king as with the lack of recognition for YHWH's kingship. The vision of Judges is never one of autonomy or radical equality but rather one of radical dependance on a sovereign God (178)....Doing what is right in our own eyes rather than in YHWH's eyes is the root of all our sin. This was the sin of Eve and of Adam. By ending the book with this refrain, the author of Judges is making clear that sin remains dominant, and indeed has grown in domination during this period....as we read the book of Judges, we are to identify with Israel's sin (192)." Judges invites the reader to see this theological reality play itself out in every generation and to call all to the immediate awareness of the one true King.

17. This line comes from the brilliant pastor and cultural commentator, Mark Sayers.

18. Genesis 2:25

19. The opening narrative of Genesis introduces us to a few Hebrew word plays before this one. For example Adam (*adam*) is formed from the ground (*adamah*) (see Genesis 2:7) and the woman (*ishah*) is taken from the man (*ish*) (see Genesis 2:23). I specifically was exposed to the *arum/arumim* wordplay from Carol A. Newsome's article "Common Ground: An Ecological Reading of Genesis 2-3" in the book *The Earth Story in Genesis* (Sheffield: Sheffield Academic Press, 2000), 67-68.

20. Alan Noble, *Disruptive Witness: Speaking Truth in a Distracted Age* (Downers Grove: InterVarsity Press, 2018), 38. My point here is obviously not that Adam and Eve lived in a secular age but that the secular age we now inhabit shares great continuity with the deep issue of our ancestors. Wright in *Here Are Your Gods* makes this exact connection, "The profoundly simple narrative of Genesis 3 portrays in graphic imagery a momentous historical turn in human history and also captures the very essence of the sin we continue to commit ever since.... It is the idolatry of the self (100)."

21. This is the point Dietrich Bonhoeffer basically makes in *Ethics* (New York: Touchstone, 1955), "Instead of seeing God, man sees himself (Gen. 3:7). Man percieves himself in disunion with God and with men....Shame is man's ineffaceable recollection of his estrangement from the origin.... Man is ashamed because he has lost something which is essential to his original character (24)." Humanity had lost an essential part of themselves in this process.

Father

1. This is why 20th century pastor and theologian A.W. Tozer's words are so pointed. He began in his short but jam-packed book about the fundamental character and nature of God called *The Knowledge of the Holy* (New York: HarperOne, 1961) with this concept, "What comes into our minds when we think about God is the most important thing about us (1)." When you first think of God as Father, what first comes into your mind? This first fundamental thought will shape not just what you believe about God but who you become in the process.

2. I added "her."

3. J.B. Phillips, *Your God is Too Small* (New York: The MacMillan Company, 1960), 14.

4. I added this as I am really trying to hit home that Jesus' original audience had #daddyissues.

5. I added this.

6. Phillips, *Your God is Too Small*, 17.

7. This takes us into the realm of what is called worship. Our picture of God is so central because *we become what we worship*. The brilliant David Foster Wallace so aptly put it in his commencement speech at Kenyon College, "In the day-to-day trenches of adult life, there is actually no such thing as atheism. There is no such thing as not worshipping. Everybody worships. The only choice we get is what to worship." Every one of us worships something or someone and what we worship will be the end to which we become.

8. Exodus 34:6-7

9. Genesis 2:9

10. Genesis 2:25. To be clear, the problem is not that Adam and Eve are naked (as they were naked before eating of the tree) but their own perception of their nakedness. As Simon Cozens and Christoph Ochs in *"Have You No Shame?" An Overlooked Theological Category as Interpretative Key in Genesis 3 (Journal of Theological Interpretation*, Vol. 13, No. 2, 2019) points out, "How did 'naked but not ashamed' become 'naked but ashamed'? Clearly their nakedness did not change (cf. 2:25 to 3:7); what changed was their perception of each other (193)." The narrative key for unlocking the point of this story is not found in a simple statement of being (naked) because humans were naked since the beginning but how humans perceive nakedness upon eating from the tree, which is what I am referring to as identity.

11. Identity is something that is meant to be given to us externally by God. As Cozens and Ochs write in *"Have You*

No Shame?" that upon listening to the serpent and "gaining an independent source of moral judgements changed both humanity's destiny and its source of self-evaluation. Ultimately it seems that identity is something that comes to us externally as creatures; it is always received from another. When the vertical relationship was severed, the horizontal stepped in its place. But deriving one's identity from horizontal relationships is a process that is constantly fraught with status anxiety and doubt, leading to a universal dissatisfaction (197)." Hence, why when any individual lowers their eyes from God to self it leads to continuing depths of identity confusion. This is a deep human tendency as Cozens in *Looking Shame in the Eye* (London: InterVarsity Press, 2019) observes, "….ever since Adam, our defence against shame has been to try to manipulate the image of ourselves that we portray to others," a process referred to as "*identity curation* (52)." Our ancestors were awoken to and conceived nakedness in a new way leading to a new identity based in self and the lies of the Serpent.

12. Understanding the horizontal and vertical dimension in the story is vital for our understanding and application. Cozens and Ochs in *"Have You No Shame?"* observe that Adam and Eve would make "for themselves fig-leaf coverings before God appeared on the scene. Their eyes were opened, and they felt the desire to cover themselves up. Given the narrative has already linked nakedness and (lack of) shame in the context of their relationship with another, it seems reasonable to read this shame reaction to nakedness in exactly the same context (194-195)….Genesis makes abundantly clear that shame is firstly a human problem (2:25; 3:7-8, 10, 21; 4:5b, 6); humanity has changed, not God (196)." This narrative invites us to see the dramatic ramifications of human autonomy that affects first our horizontal relationship with others as well as our vertical relationship with God.

13. Genesis 3:14+17

14. Brene Brown, *The Power of Vulnerability* (https://www. ted.com/talks/brene_brown_the_power_of_vulnerability/ up-next?language=en). Brene Brown has done lots of valuable work around the topic of shame. In-response to shame, she generally directs people to practice deliberate authenticity as well as self-compassion. My main concern is not that these are vital practices but that they are not sufficient within themselves as they ultimately end in *self*. As Cozens in *Looking Shame in the Eye* writes, "We're *meant* to get our identity by looking up to God, not from those around us, or even by looking inside ourselves. Calvin's *Institutes* begins by saying 'that man never attains to a true self-knowledge until he has previously contemplated the face of God, and come down after such contemplation to look into himself'. As we look upward to God, and hear his voice speaking out his evaluation of us -- created 'in our image, in our likeness', 'very good' (Genesis 1:26, 31) -- we get our true identity from him (56)." Point being, I do value Brown's writing but her solutions will relate to many of my critiques of modern forms of cultural formation in my next chapter, *Telos*.

15. Galatians 3:16, Romans 16:20, Revelation 12:9, 1 John 3:8-10

16. Genesis 3:21. Claus Westermann in his work, *Genesis*, Volume 1 (Edinburgh: T & T, 1995) summarizes this scene well, "The last action of the creator towards his creature before expelling him from the garden is an action of care and concern….the creator protects his creature while putting them at a distance, and the protective action accompanies them on the way (269)."

17. R.W.L. Moberly, *The Theology of the Book of Genesis* (Old Testament Theology) (New York: Cambridge University Press, 2009), 86.

Telos

1. This story is from: https://www.nytimes.com/2019/01/31/technology/apple-blocks-facebook.html.

2. Daniel J. Siegel, *Mindsight: The New Science of Personal Transformation* (New York: Bantam Books, 2010), 39. Many modern scholars use the term "brain" in a wider sense than just our brains. Scholars at UCLA including Siegel acknowledge this in their use of "brain" as "it's important to remember that the activity of what we're calling the 'brain' is not just in our heads….the heart has an extensive network of nerves that process complex information and relay data upward to the brain in the skull. So, too, do the intestines, and all the other major organ systems of the body (43)." In their use, one's brain encompasses the functions of the whole person, which actually aligns quite nicely with biblical truth as the Bible uses the term "heart" in a similar manner. Throughout this book, my use of "heart" is similar to how modern neuroscientists use the term "brain." I like using the heart instead as it aligns better with the biblical tradition and connotes more than just the power of thoughts but also the central role of our desires.

3. I added "insert habit you want to change here." This quote is from Charles Duhigg, *The Power of Habit: Why We Do What We Do and How to Change* (New York: Random House Publishers, 2014), 270. This is a solid book but not my favorite book on habits. I would highly recommend *Atomic Habits* by James Clear. He really pushes past mere habit loop hacking and goes into how identity is central to our formation.

4. For more on the importance of developing a craft, I would highly recommend Cal Newport's work, *So Good They Can't Ignore You* (London: Piatkus, 2012). He really challenges the whole "follow your passions" ethic in our cultural moment and how star performers actually got to where they are.

5. Malcolm Gladwell, *Outliers: The Story of Success* (New York: Little, Brown and Company, 2008), 40. Daniel J. Levitin, *This Is Your Brain on Music: The Science of a Human Obsession* (New York: Dutton, 2006), 197.

6. Jeffrey M. Schwartz and Rebecca Gladding, *You Are Not Your Brain* (New York: Avery, 2012), 39.

7. This centrality of the heart points us to the central place of *desire* in our spiritual growth. Without a proper understanding of the role of the heart and inner life, we are destined to have truncated views of formation focused merely on conscious practices instead of the central role of unconscious desires. Smith aptly writes in *You Are What You Love*, "But the telos we live toward is not something that we primarily know or believe or think about; rather, our telos is what we want, what we long for, what we crave. It is less an ideal that we have ideas about and more a vision of 'the good life' that we desire

(11)." Central to the cultivation of one's heart is the role of our desires which point towards some telos, whether through intentional or unintentional practice.

8. Formation is deeply embedded within the human consciousness - regardless of one's own religious beliefs. Dallas Willard observes this reality in *Renovation of the Heart*, "In any case, we may be sure of this: the formation and, later, transformation of the inner life of man, from which our outer existence flows, is an inescapable human problem. Spiritual formation, without regard to any specifically religious context or tradition, is the process by which the human spirit or will is given a definite "form" or character. It is a process that happens to everyone (19)." As Willard observes, every person is going through the process of formation. Day-in and day-out all of us are becoming something, whether through intentional or unintentional formation; and this formation leads us to some end which we live for as the fundamental orientation of our lives - a telos.

9. Genesis 2:7

10. Genesis 2:24

11. Genesis 2:9. This observation came from the brilliant professor and theologian Tim Mackie. Nahum Sarna in *Understanding Genesis: The Heritage of Biblical Israel* (New York: Schocken Books, 1970) makes a similar point, "The same is true, and even more so, in the treatment of the two trees. They possess no magical properties which operate independently of God. They are in no wise outside of the divine realm, and their mysterious powers do not exist apart from the will of God (25)."

12. Genesis 11:4 - this is the NIV translation.

13. Genesis 2:17

14. Genesis 3:4

15. L. Michael Morales articulates the ramifications of this all beautifully in his work *Exodus Old and New* (Downers Grove: InterVarsity Press, 2020), "The quest for eternal significance through accomplishment, for security derived from power, for lasting reality by rootedness in a place; the search for meaning and the ache for hope; the undermining of every happy occasion through the profound awareness of its fleeting nature; in short, the longing to find a home so as finally to come home--these are all the inescapable burdens of life in exile from God, of the human soul turned in on itself. Apart from life with the Creator, creation itself groans in futility, stripped of meaning, emptied of significance, void of purpose. Severed from the fountain of life, humanity's inner longings and deepest desires find no ultimate objective, *no telos*---neither goal or guide. And then long before we have tasted it, life runs out--and to dust we return (16)."

16. John Sailhamer in *The Pentateuch as Narrative* (Grand Rapids: Zondervan, 1992) makes this exact connection to the opening narrative of Genesis: "The man and the woman, who had been created "like God" in the beginning (1:26), found themselves, after the Fall, curiously "like God"--but no longer "with God" in the Garden. In this subtle verbal interchange the author has shown that human happiness does not consist in being "like God" but rather being "with God," enjoying the blessings of his presence (110)."

17. Italicized added. Willard, *The Spirit of the Disciplines*, 138.

Presence

1. Brother Lawerence, *The Practice of the Presence of God* (Grand Rapids: Spire Books, 1967), 30. I also would highly recommend Tish Harrison Warren's *Liturgy of the Ordinary* (Downers Grove: InterVarsity Press, 2016). It is a more so modern exploration of how the practices and Presence fit within our normal rhythms and routines.

2. Leviticus 26:11

3. When you get into the weeds of the Tabernacle, it begins to extremely evident its connection to Eden. We see the 1) Stationing of the Cherubim. These are guardian-like figures used throughout the Bible. After the reference in Genesis 3:24, the next time we will see them referenced is in the Holy of Holies in the Tabernacle (Ex. 26:1, 31; 25:18-22) which is the place where God's presence will dwell among His people. We also see 2) the flaming sword. The Holy of Holies is guarded by them (Exod. 26:1, 31) and fashioned on the atonement lid of the ark (Exod. 25:18-22). Flames are also a sign of the presence of God. We see 3) God's presence dwelling on the western side of the tabernacle (Exodus 25:8) which points us to the eastern/western journey of God's people in Eden seen in the previous chapter. Finally 4) the tabernacles rooms were designed with a tree-like lampstand at the center and with trees all around that were crafted like the tree of life (Exodus 25:31-40 + 1 Kings 6:29).

4. Leviticus 26:12

5. Leviticus 26:12

6. John 1:14

7. Tim Keller, *Encounters with Jesus* (New York: Dutton, 2013), 3.

8. John 1:14

9. John 1:14

10. G.K. Beale, *The Temple and the Church's Mission: A Biblical Theology of the Dwelling Place of God* (Downers Grove: InterVarsity Press, 2004), 195. In the midst of publishing this book, I came across Richard Bauckham's *Who is God? Key Moments of Biblical Revelation* (Grand Rapids: Baker Academic, 2020). The theological flow of this chapter is masterfully summarized by Bauckham in pages 27-32.

11. Hebrews 12:2

12. Revelation 21:1

13. Recommended resources for reframing one's understanding of Revelation + the end times would include: 1) Michael Gorman's *Reading Revelation Responsibly* (Eugene: Cascade Books, 2011), 2) Eugene Peterson's *Reversed Thunder* (New York: HarperOne, 1988) and 3) *Surprised by Hope* by N.T. Wright (New York: HarperOne, 2008).

14. Revelation 21:3

15. Revelation 22:1-2. If you want more on how this motif of a return to Eden is seen throughout the entire biblical story (especially in the tabernacle/temple), I highly recommend L. Michael Morales' *Who Shall Ascend the Mountain of the Lord? A biblical theology of Leviticus* (Downers Grove: InterVarsity Press, 2015).

16. Revelation 21:3

17. Smith, *You Are What You Love*, 90.

18. This is a quote from the Westminster Shorter Catechism.

19. Antoine de Saint-Exupéry, *The Wisdom of the Sands* (New York: Harcourt Brace, 1950).

Here and Now

1. I am using the framework of the 4 S's of Sabbath, simplicity, slowing and silence from John Mark Comer's book, *The Ruthless Elimination of Hurry* (Colorado Springs: WaterBrook, 2019).

2. Matthew 11:28-30, The Message.

About

Well, this is where I tell you *all* the good things about me. The easiest part of the book for an Enneagram 3, (recovering) performer like myself. I'm going to keep this simple because this is only partly a competition (totally is).

I am a *husband + father.* I am married to Hilary and have two kiddos, Ephraim + Abram.

I am a *pastor* at Mill Creek Foursquare Church. This is my vocation and I have given my life to help people understand God's breathtaking story found in the biblical scriptures.

I am a *Seattleite.* Born and raised in the PNW.

I am a *bible nerd.* I hold a Masters in Biblical and Theological Studies from Western Seminary and two undergraduate degrees in Religious Studies + Business from the University of Puget Sound.

I am a *follower* of Jesus and a practitioner of His way in the world. Probably my most fundamental description of who and what I'm all about.

Made in the USA
Coppell, TX
04 February 2021

49642530R10125